GETTING A LIFE
Living Your Call

Douglas B. Miller

Foreword by
David Faber

The Reader's Press

Hillsboro, Kansas

Library of Congress Cataloging-in-Publication Data
Miller, Douglas B.
Getting a life: living your call / Douglas B. Miller. — 1st ed.

Library of Congress Control Number: 2016947292
ISBN 978-0-9851762-4-2 (paper)

19 20 / 10 9 8 7 6 5 4 3

Contents

Abbreviations

cf.	compare	Jon.	Jonah
ch.	chapter	Judg.	Judges
Col.	Colossians	Mal.	Malachi
Cor.	Corinthians	Matt.	Matthew
Deut.	Deuteronomy	Message	The Message
Eccl.	Ecclesiastes		Version
e.g.	for example	Mic.	Micah
emph.	emphasis	NIV	New International
Eph.	Ephesians		Version
esp.	especially	NLT	New Living
ESV	English Standard		Translation
	Version	NRSV	New Revised
Exod.	Exodus		Standard Version
Gal.	Galatians	Num.	Numbers
Gen.	Genesis	Pet.	Peter
Hab.	Habakkuk	Phil.	Philippians
HCSB	Holman Christian	Ps./Pss.	Psalm/Psalms
	Standard Bible	Rev.	Revelation
Heb.	Hebrews	Rom.	Romans
i.e.	that is	Sam.	Samuel
Isa.	Isaiah	Thess.	Thessalonians
Jer.	Jeremiah	Tim.	Timothy

Foreword

The fox knows a great many things,
but the hedgehog knows one great thing.

So wrote the Greek poet Archilochus in about 650 BCE. Nobody knows what he really meant; all that has been handed down is this isolated fragment. But it is a suggestive saying. Is it better to be the fox and know a lot? Or is it better to be the hedgehog and know one great thing?

Everybody likes being an expert. And everybody—or almost everybody—has something about which he or she *is* an expert. Sometimes expertise is a personal interest; you might be an expert on the history and geography of the Star Wars universe or an expert on all things about the Phoenix Suns or on the career of The Avett Brothers. Other times one's expertise is professional. You might be an expert on the chemistry of the onion or on the history of the black press or the music of Bach. The desire for expertise is both a natural feature of human curiosity and a professional expectation for most people; sometimes our expertise is a hobby and sometimes it is a job. For some people it is both.

Of course being *an* expert is different from being *the* expert. To be an expert is to know a great deal about some aspect of the world; it is to know more than most people know about that subject. To be *the* expert is to know more than anybody else about that subject. It is like being a great athlete or a great musician; one can be *an* expert tennis player while acknowledging that there are better players or be *an* expert pianist while aware that there are better musicians.

The Fox as Expert
Like the fox, an expert knows a great many things. A college education, for example, should help you to become an expert.

Sometimes the education provides the student with an impressive array of practical skills. This is the strength of technical schools and professional degrees. A student of welding or of accounting is able to jump right into a job, which benefits both the employer and the new employee. A weakness of a narrow development of expertise, however, is that our world is constantly, swiftly changing. Unlike the relatively recent past in which a trade could be handed down from generation to generation nearly unchanged, the fast-changing pace of technical innovation can quickly render one's expertise obsolete. This kind of expertise, while valuable, is a surface expertise. Many students (and parents) think only on the surface, but this is short-sighted. Taking a longer view, students should seek an education that also provides a deeper kind of expertise.

A deeper expertise involves knowing not only the specific information about a subject, but also knowing other things that are around the subject. A deeper expertise knows the history of the subject, the philosophical presuppositions behind the subject, and the ideas that animate the subject. A deeper expertise understands the psychology and sociology involved as well as the role that the subject plays in the imagination of a culture.

For instance, a deeper expertise in accounting knows not only the current tax code but also what the country is trying to accomplish with the tax code, what taxes used to be like, and what some of the issues are regarding the fairness of the tax code. This deeper expertise understands the motivations that make it more (or less) likely that people will comply with tax laws. It understands how the culture as a whole feels about taxes.

Similarly, a deeper expertise in baseball understands more than just the rules of the game and the current standings. It might know the physics of what makes a pitch curve and the mathematics of the probability that an infield shift will be successful. Even deeper, this expertise may know the place of baseball in the American psyche. Such deeper expertise knows how baseball both reflects and shapes many attitudes in our culture. It knows the role that Jackie Robinson's breaking of the color barrier in Major League Baseball played in the larger civil rights movement. Likewise, a liberal arts education can show a person how to think about a subject from a variety of perspectives—scientific, philosophical, literary, historical, psychological, and social. The innovation and adaptability that are so prized in contemporary life and work arise out of this deeper expertise.

A perplexing feature of contemporary life is that there are so many experts, yet they don't agree with one another. One expert—or purported expert—says that recent average increases in temperature over the world are due to human factors and calls for significant policy changes. Another expert—or purported expert—argues that the rise in temperature is part of a normal cycle and advises that no policy changes are necessary. At its best, a liberal arts education not only helps a student become an expert, but it hones a student's ability to distinguish among experts, to answer the question "Whom should I trust?"

Further, a better education not only helps you develop a deeper expertise; it more importantly helps you learn *how* to develop this deeper expertise. By studying a wide variety of disciplines—such as literature, psychology, mathematics, history, and philosophy—you learn how to ask a greater variety of valuable questions that enable you to better appraise the surrounding culture.

Knowing One Great Thing

So far, we have been describing a fox—or, perhaps, two kinds of fox. We have been describing someone who knows a great many things and who knows how to learn and assess many more things. Both of these are important and valuable. Many people are satisfied with being one of these two kinds of fox. But an excellent liberal arts education can provide a depth of expertise even deeper than the two just described.

Being the cleverest of foxes is not enough. An education should also help a student to become a hedgehog; an education should help a student understand one great thing. Think about the Harry Potter stories that have been so popular in recent years. The key difference between Dumbledore and Voldemort is their vision of the one great thing. Voldemort views magic as a way of exercising power for his own goals. The purpose of magic for him is to subjugate Muggles to magicians and to subjugate other magicians to himself. Ultimately, he sought magical power to make himself invincible and immortal. Dumbledore, on the other hand, had a vision that downplayed the differences between wizards and Muggles, and saw magic as a means for benefitting both communities.

Many in contemporary education believe that there is no "one great thing" and thus reject both Voldemort and Dumbledore. Many in academe hold that there is no grand story that makes sense out of life; there is no story that provides a context that makes one's life and deep expertise meaningful and purposeful.

This is where a Christian liberal arts education stands out. A Christian liberal arts education deepens a student's understanding of the world as a place that is created by a good and loving God who has made humans the caretakers of that world. It provides the "one great thing" as well as discernment for evaluating competing claims.

The Value of the Hedgehog

For the reasons given above, you need to be both a hedgehog and a fox. The one great thing—and for me this means seeing life through the lens of faith in Jesus—interprets our experience and guides our choices.

One hard truth is that nobody knows how their life will turn out. Some will build a business that becomes more profitable than they ever could have imagined; some will lose a child to cancer or some other disease; some will choose a quiet life and have neither great success nor great pain. The one great thing, the grand story, can help you make sense of your life, along with whatever success or suffering may come.

In addition to helping you interpret your experiences, the one great thing can guide the choices that you make. If you are in college right now, you are likely thinking about a job and a career. If not, you may be considering whether the direction you are headed is the best one. A life of following Jesus may lead a person to ask the question, "What is God asking me to do? What is my role in this grand story?" As you read this book you will be invited to think about such questions in connection with God's calling; those following Jesus will be asked to think about what God is calling them to do. You will also be introduced to a disciplined reflection known as a personal mission statement.

In my context at a Christian liberal arts college we believe that a student should be both a fox and a hedgehog. It is my hope and expectation that this book will help you to become just that, to learn a great many things as well as one great thing.

— David Faber
Hillsboro, Kansas

Preface

More than some publishing projects, this book has benefited from the collaborative feedback of many persons for which I am extremely grateful. My thanks go to those who read earlier drafts and gave comments: Blake Atkinson, Rick Bartlett, Christina Bucher, Melissa Cairns, Cody Coleman, Kalee Cross, Joseph Donnell, Omar Galvan, Kelly Gomez, Ted Grimsrud, Taylor Hurd, Susan Jantzen, Brandon Johnson, Jeremy Johnson, Lynn Jost, Paul Keim, Sheila Klassen-Wiebe, Kristen Marble, Aaron Miller, Daniel Miller, Manuel Miranda-Cortez, Lydia Padilla, Holly Swartzendruber, and Kaleigh Troxell. I especially owe a debt of gratitude to members of my department, who gave thoughtful critiques and to whom the book is dedicated: David Faber, Del Gray, and Wendell Loewen. Additional thanks are due to David Faber for contributing the foreword, to Joel Klaassen and Aaron Miller for technical assistance, and to members of Derek Hamm's graphic design course (and to Derek himself) for the cover design and suggestions for the interior: Laura Pankratz, Trenton Parrish, Rebecca Strobridge, Bailey Clark, Mariah Kliewer, and David Witt. I am grateful to Aleen Ratzlaff for her excellent copy editing.

All of these have helped to make this a better book. I am responsible for the limitations that remain.

—*Douglas B. Miller*
Hillsboro, Kansas

Introduction

This book is intended primarily for young adults and others in Western and especially North American cultures who are thinking about career and other future-oriented decisions. It is written from a self-consciously Christian perspective, but with the awareness that there is diversity within the Christian family and not all would present the Christian faith as done here. The author also hopes it will be inviting for those from other traditions or who are still making decisions about their own worldview. Whoever you are, it is designed to help you better understand yourself, where you're headed, what choices you've already made (often without knowing it), and some possible decisions you might want to think about. It has to do with finding purpose in life, what and whom to believe, what good life to aim for, and, as a result, what job or profession to choose to help pay the bills. Or maybe more than just paying the bills.

Each chapter introduces an issue, helps you to discover what you already believe and do about that issue, and gives you some additional possibilities to think about. Often a Christian perspective or proposal is presented for illustration and for your consideration. If you have already embraced a Christian worldview, the hope is that you will understand that better in the midst of other options. If that is not your commitment, the hope is that you will understand your own approach better and why you have taken it. Even if you don't embrace a Christian worldview as a whole, you may find portions of it that align with your own thinking, which may challenge you to rethink the implications of what you believe.

The book is about making sense of life and work. At its heart is a Christian concept known as "vocation." The English word derives from the Latin *vocare*, meaning "to call," and the concept is found in both the Old and New Testament of the

Bible, reflected especially in the Hebrew *qara'* and the Greek *kaleo*. In this book, we will use the words *vocation, calling,* and *mission* interchangeably. The caller is God. The one called is a human being, such as when God called the man who was hiding in the garden, asking "Where are you?" (Gen. 3:9). More significantly for our purposes are examples such as God calling to Moses from a burning bush (Exod. 3:4), calling the boy Samuel (1 Sam. 3), and calling Mary, the mother of Jesus (Luke 1:26-38). In each case the person is given an assignment. Likewise, Jesus calls disciples to follow him (Matt. 4:21; 9:13; Mark 1:20).

Today many voices call for our attention: voices of friends, voices of advertisers, voices of society, voices from our false self. For the Christian, vocation means discerning which of these, if any, are from God or aligned with God's values. For those adopting a different worldview, one's sense of purpose may be framed differently, but it will still mean sorting through several possibilities to find the one or ones that seem to fit best.

To understand one's calling, it will be helpful to know about a number of interrelated issues. Chapter 1 introduces and invites you to a life of **adventure** as you explore who you are and where you are headed. Chapter 2 is concerned with certain lenses for seeing known as **worldviews**. The third chapter provides some practical indicators and offers a process for understanding your **identity** and **purpose** as well as avoiding some traps; it proposes a **mission statement** as a way of articulating your life goals. In chapter 4, we consider what it means to have **faith** in something or someone as well as distortions of faith. Chapter 5 presents some specific elements of a Christian worldview and four themes (**God's Design**) that summarize God's interaction with people and to which we are called. Chapter 6 examines the place of **community** in a life of purpose and the essential role of the Christian community.

Chapter 7 studies how to find the right **clues** while traveling through a culture characterized as Postmodern, and chapter 8 presents Christian considerations for finding **truth**. The focus of the ninth chapter is on discerning **what is good** and

how the study of ethics can help. Chapter 10 explores and critiques a Postmodern parable concerning its **vision of the good
life**. Chapter 11 takes a look at the ideological crisis of our time
and **six models for engaging** one's **culture**.

In chapter 12, we consider the role of **work** as presented in
the Bible. The thirteenth chapter invites you to consider how to
integrate your personal and corporate sense of calling with the
possibility of a **job** and **profession**. Finally, chapter 14 describes how serving God and people through our vocation is
used by God to bring growth and blessing to our lives, including **virtues** essential for our calling. It ends with a challenge to
carry out your **mission**.

A major assumption in these pages is that your life will
never be truly fulfilling until you find ways you can contribute
to the needs of our present era. The book's intent is to help you
find purpose for your life as you consider God's goals for
human beings.

Part 1
Finding Our Way

After several unsuccessful attempts, the bush plane finally clears the runway and heads into the frozen wilds of the Yukon. Chillingly beautiful snow-covered mountains spread out below as the pilot and his passenger soar toward the outpost where Tyler will spend the next six months monitoring the habits of Arctic wolves. As he views the scene outside the plane, Tyler begins to have serious doubts about his ability to survive in such an environment. Rosie, a man who has been through such a trip many times, suspects that Tyler has concerns about his piloting abilities in such terrain. So he assures him that he "feels his way through these mountains blindfolded all the time."

Rosie, on the other hand, wants to know what would bring Tyler on such a daring expedition: Is it manganese? oil? gold? When Tyler is hesitant to say, the pilot becomes a bit philosophical and laments the struggle of those seeking their fortune in the north, scratching to find "that one crack in the ground, so that they never have to scratch again." Yet Rosie seems even more distressed about those who play it safe, who sit at home watching television, bored to death.

At this point, the single engine on the plane begins to sputter and finally stops. As the aircraft drifts and loses altitude among jagged and ice-covered mountain peaks, Tyler starts to panic, frantically asking Rosie "What's wrong?!" Rosie quickly instructs Tyler to take the plane's controls, rummages desperately through his tool box, yells in frustration, then pauses. "Boredom, Tyler," says Rosie. "Boredom, that's what's wrong." Then, just before he opens the door of the plane to hang outside and bang vigorously on a frozen fuel line, he asks, "How do you beat boredom?" Holding up a wrench victoriously, he answers his own question: "Adventure!"[1]

Life is meant to be an adventure, yet many people today don't sense that excitement. Deep inside all people, from those who live in luxury to those who struggle to overcome trauma or to have the basics of life, there can be an emptiness, a lack of engagement with the essence of life. Adventure, the way I intend here, means to embrace that essence, to brave the unknown, to be open to risk and danger. It demands courage and involves challenge, figuring out who you are and what you've got inside of you, what you are capable of. It often involves confusion and uncertainty, getting things partly right, making some successes, sometimes great successes. Yes, adventure demands courage, and courage isn't the lack of fear—courage is doing something significant even though you may be afraid.

Who Wants a Bland Life?

In most cases, people hope for a life that is interesting and not completely predictable. It is true that we define excitement for ourselves in different ways. Also, a calm life will be more appealing if we have experienced tragedy or some other trauma. But at least as we start out, we hope for adventure, something new, a risk that is worth taking. In fact, no one can live a completely safe life. We all experience risk, uncertainty, and difficulty. But there are voices and pressures around us urging us to play it safe.

Of course, nothing is wrong in itself with being safe, and nothing is commendable about taking high risks just for a brief thrill. Yet a life spent seeking only that which is safe can be quite dull. Perhaps surprisingly, the Christian church has sometimes developed a fortress mentality and encouraged its members to be "good." And by *good* they often mean to stop doing certain things while very little positive is promoted—

except perhaps to be faithful to one's family and to serve the church.

This may leave the impression that a life of faith is a dull life. However, even a superficial acquaintance with the lives of those recorded in the Bible shows quite the opposite. Abraham and Sarah? Isaac and Rebekah? Joseph? Moses? What about Ruth? Esther? David? Elijah? Jeremiah? And Mary? Jesus? His disciples? The Apostle Paul? Uncertainty, yes; confusion, often; danger, many times. Nothing, however, that would suggest boredom, although doubtless some days were more dull than exciting. When these people of faith signed on to follow God's call, they found the antidote to a bland life: Adventure!

I suggest that *adventure* is a legitimate way to frame the life for which God created us. Not a life of comfort, nor a life of certainty, not even a life of successes that we can always count on. But a life of faithfulness that embraces adventure as its normal by-product. In part, this is because human beings were created to participate in God's battle against evil, a battle that requires courage, strategy, creativity, initiative; also a battle that should be fought in certain ways and not other ways.

If the message is primarily to withdraw, to avoid danger, to play it safe—there is no adventure. And one of the predictable results of losing adventure is boredom, a symptom that we have not fully engaged life and its opportunities. All that zest, all that motivation—which, of course, certainly *can* be misdirected—is told to calm down and go to sleep. We become insipid people, of little use to God, others, or ourselves.

I have had the privilege several times to travel to the Holy Land and to visit places where people lived that we read about in the Bible, where they walked, worked, prayed, and worshiped. Reflecting on their stories in the land where they lived and traveled makes it a bit more real: the unknown, risk and danger, courage, excitement, confusion, and uncertainty.

Notice, for example, that when God knocks Paul down with a bright light, calls him to a particular mission, and blinds him for several days, he sends another person (Ananias) to give Paul a message (Acts 9). The message is *not*, "Tell Paul that any time he meets trouble I will always eliminate it for him, every time he faces enemies, I will remove them." No, Ananias is directed to tell Paul how much Paul will have to suffer for Jesus' sake. And we then watch Paul experience just that: being attacked and nearly killed several times, on occasion living poor and hungry, enduring shipwreck, and submitting to a chronic physical ailment. Yet we also find some powerful things happening through Paul: people are healed, people are brought to Christ, churches are planted and strengthened, and leaders are trained. Here is one of Paul's comments about this life of adventure:

> Do you think anyone is going to be able to drive a wedge between us and Christ's love for us? There is no way! Not trouble, not hard times, not hatred, not hunger, not homelessness, not bullying threats, not backstabbing . . . . None of this fazes us because Jesus loves us. (Rom. 8:35, 37 Message)

This is written by someone who knows he is in a battle, that good things as well as bad things will come, and he is confident that the outcome will eventually be good. *But* he hasn't seen that outcome yet; he will have to live out this adventure one experience at a time.

A group called Christian Peacemaker Teams is made of people who sense a call to confront situations of injustice using nonviolent methods; they use tactics consistent with Jesus' life and teachings. For a number of years, CPT members have taken up residence in Hebron, a city in the West Bank where there are often tensions and occasional outbreaks of violence. On a wall in their (very spartan) apartment, among other encouraging quotations, I saw posted Acts 4:29, a prayer prayed by early Christians who had been warned not to do what Jesus asked them to do:

> Now, Lord, consider their threats and enable your servants to speak your word with great boldness.[2]

This prayer aligns with a life of adventure: a concern not primarily for safety but for strength to faithfully carry out God's mission. Likewise, we should not be surprised if identifying and responding to the call on our own lives should mean doing something with risk, something not quite certain, heading into unknown territory, perhaps facing opposition.

Confidence along the Way

I conclude with reference to another story in its dramatized version.[3] If you have read Tolkien's *Lord of the Rings*, or have seen one or more of the films, you know that this is a sort of anti-quest drama, a journey to destroy an evil and powerful artifact (a ring) rather than to find one, somewhat as if Indiana Jones would risk his life to give away the Ark of the Covenant! Along the way, the characters discover important things about each other and about themselves. In the midst of the mines of Moria, Frodo becomes fearful when he learns that the group is being pursued by a dangerous creature named Gollum, who previously lost the ring to Bilbo. Gandalf, the wise older guide, gives some counsel. In the film, we hear the following:

> Frodo: It's a pity Bilbo didn't kill [Gollum] when he had the chance.

> Gandalf: Pity? It was pity that stayed Bilbo's hand. Many that live deserve death, and some that die deserve life. Can you give it to them, Frodo? Do not be too eager to deal out death and judgment. Even the very wise cannot see all ends. My heart tells me that Gollum has some part to play yet for good or ill before this is over. The pity of Bilbo may rule the fate of many.

> Frodo: I wish the ring had never come to me. I wish none of this had happened.

> Gandalf: So do all who live to see such times. But that is not for them to decide. All we have to decide is what to do with the time that is given to us. There are other forces at work in this world, Frodo, besides the will of evil. Bilbo was *meant* to find the ring, in which case you also were *meant* to have it. And that is an encouraging thought.

As Gandalf realizes, we cannot control what is going to happen around us. What is asked of us is to respond to the issues and challenges that come our way. If we are alert, we will recognize encouraging signs that we can have confidence to persevere.

The conversation between Frodo and Gandalf introduces another consideration. In the process of our mission, we do well to cultivate mercy toward those who disappoint us and even seek to harm us, as Joseph in the Bible said to his brothers who had tried to kill him,

> You intended to harm me, but God intended it for good to accomplish what is now being done, the saving of many lives. (Gen. 50:20)

Even when others try to harm us, we can trust God to work good out of it. Thus we can have confidence that there is a task for us to fulfill, and we can be encouraged that there will be resources available for us to accomplish it.

Questions for Reflection and Discussion
1. Do you find life to be worth living? Why or why not? What answers does this chapter provide? Continue to reflect on this issue as you read through subsequent chapters.
2. Evaluate the term *adventure* to describe life. What is accurate or helpful, inaccurate or not helpful about that term?
3. Do you tend to think of God's call or the life Jesus invites people to live as exciting and adventurous? Or more bland and uninteresting? What contributes to your view?

Suggestions for Further Reading
Henry T. Blackaby and Claude V. King, *Experiencing God*. Nashville, TN: Broadman and Holman, 1994.
Os Guinness, *The Call: Finding and Fulfilling the Central Purpose of Your Life*. Nashville, TN: Word, 1998.
Kathleen Kern, *In Harm's Way: A History of Christian Peacemaker Teams*. Eugene, OR: Cascade, 2009.

CHAPTER 2
Seeing the Road Ahead

Hikers, explorers, and hunters often use special glasses, binoculars, or night vision goggles to see what lies ahead. Likewise, as we journey through this adventurous life, we need to be able to see what is going on. In some ways, a worldview is like a lens through which we see life. Just as the right glasses can give us a clear vision of the road on which we travel, so the right worldview can give us a clear perspective on life. James Sire defines it this way:

> A worldview is a commitment, a fundamental orientation of the heart, that can be expressed as a story or as a set of presuppositions (assumptions which may be true, partially true, or entirely false) which we hold (consciously or subconsciously, consistently or inconsistently) about the basic constitution of reality, and that provides the foundation on which we live and move and have our being.[4]

Our worldview determines our values, organizes and interprets our world. It helps us sort out what is most important. For most of us, it continues to be under construction and revision for some time, and yet at some point it stabilizes into something we rely on every day. Sire emphasizes that a worldview is not just a set of assumptions picked up at an intellectual smorgasbord, or chosen like an item of clothing. Rather, it is an orientation of one's true inner self in ways of which we may not be aware. It manifests itself in our behavior, perhaps even more significantly than the way we think. A worldview is something passed on from one person or group to others.[5]

One good strategy is to become aware of our worldview and then to allow it to be critiqued for accuracy and soundness. If you want to discover someone's worldview, or your own, you can consider the following:

- What the person *believes*, asking several basic questions about what he or she values most in life
- Which *stories* are most central and meaningful to the person
- Which *symbols* are most central and meaningful to the person
- How the person *acts*, the choices they make, the priorities by which they live

Basic questions help distinguish one worldview from another. We all assume some kind of answer to each of these questions, even if we have not carefully developed a coherent worldview for ourselves. Here are some examples of what are typically called *existential* questions because they concern the basic dimensions of our existence: What is the prime reality — the really real? What is a human being? What happens to a person at death? Why is it possible to know anything at all? How do we know what is right and wrong? What is the meaning of human history? What is the best vision of the good life? Sire considers how answers to these questions align with a variety of worldviews.[6] The following list, not mutually exclusive, is accompanied in most cases by the answer of each worldview to the question, "What is the prime reality, the really real?" These simplifications give a hint of how each worldview sees the world, but are incomplete explanations.

Epicureanism: No one can know what actually exists. The attempt to know more puts at risk the pursuit of pleasure, which is all that is important.

Skepticism: All is subjective, there is no objective truth.

Cynicism: There is objective truth, but the meaning of life is subjective.

Naturalism: Matter and energy exist eternally and are all there is. God does not exist. The human mind has potential to discover objective reality. Two prominent forms of naturalism currently are secular humanism and Marxism.

Nihilism: Denies the ability to know anything, and thus questions the reality of existence itself.

Eastern Pantheistic Monism: "God" is the cosmos. The cosmos is everything. Examples: Some forms of Hinduism and Buddhism.

Moral Relativism: There is objective truth, but right and wrong are subjective.

Atheistic Existentialism: The prime reality is the cosmos, composed solely of matter, appearing to humans as objective on the one hand and subjective on the other. Each person has the opportunity to create his or her own meaning out of life.

Paganism: Multiple gods exist; everything else derives from them, including matter.

Deism: A God that is transcendent, a first cause, who created the universe but then left it to run on its own. God is thus not immanent, not triune, not fully personal, not sovereign over human affairs, not providential.

Judaism: God, who is holy, infinite, personal, revealed in presence and in Scripture, transcendent and immanent, omniscient, sovereign, and good. Revealed supremely in the written word, God called Israel as a servant people to bless the world.

Christian Theism: God, who is holy, infinite, personal, triune, revealed in Scripture but supremely in Jesus Christ, transcendent and immanent, omniscient, sovereign, good.

Islamic Theism: God (Allah), who is one, holy, infinite, personal, transcendent, immanent, omniscient, sovereign, and good. Revealed supremely in the word to Mohammed.

Theistic Existentialism: Affirms that God is transcendent and immanent, infinite and personal, yet the human situation is perceived as ambiguous and ambivalent, faith a total leap.

The New Age: The self is the prime reality. As human beings
grow in their awareness and grasp of this fact, the human
race is on the verge of a radical change in human nature;
even now we see harbingers of transformed humanity and
prototypes of the New Age.

Postmodernism: We cannot know what is really real. All we
know is what we construct with language.

Pluralism: The belief that two or more worldviews (or faiths)
are valid or acceptable. In the West there are two primary
forms: (1) accepting more than one path to the final goal,
and (2) a move to combine the insights and experience
from major worldviews or religions to form a new one.[7]

Narrative Representations

In addition to a list of propositions, worldviews are also represented by stories, and stories reflect worldviews. The plot line
of worldview stories gives answers to five questions that can
be related to those above: (1) Where are we? (the nature of reality), (2) Who are we? (the nature and purpose of human beings), (3) What's wrong? (how evil and brokenness are
explained), (4) What's the remedy? (what is good, how to
achieve wholeness), and (5) What time is it? (where we are in
the narrative story line).[8]

Here is one attempt at some Christian answers: (1) We are
in a universe, and on a planet, created by the one true God.
(2) We human beings are creatures, made in the image of this
God, who are appointed as guardians of the rest. (3) However,
we have gone wrong, disobeyed, sinned against this God and,
as a result, much of creation is not as God intended. (4) The
remedy has been developed by God through the people of Israel and, most significantly, through the ministry of God made
human who lived among us in Jesus of Nazareth; Jesus invited
people and continues to invite us to become his disciples and
to make more disciples in order to be part of his mission of restoration, called the "kingdom of God." (5) We are on the time-
line between Jesus' earthly ministry and when he returns. The
new creation has already begun but is not yet completed,
awaiting Jesus' second coming.

A Better Lens for a Pluralist Culture?

It is no secret that many people in our world, and likely in your neighborhood, have adopted one of several other worldviews. That is, we live in a Pluralist culture; we have pretty much accepted the fact that not everyone believes the same, even about some of the most basic aspects of what is really real. Later we will consider options for how we might relate to each other in such a context. Hopefully, what has been presented above has piqued your interest in discovering your own worldview. Perhaps you have already recognized it.

So is it possible to be sure one has the best lens through which to see life, the world, and everything? The answer to that, of course, depends on your worldview! We will return to this challenging issue a bit later. For now, let's consider some simple and necessarily simplistic considerations regarding some of the worldviews listed above.

For those who believe that pleasure (and avoiding pain) is all that life is about (*Epicureanism*), nothing is particularly illogical about such a perspective; one must consider whether intuitive indicators, some unavoidable realities, suggest otherwise. *Skeptics* claim that all truth is subjective, perceived only within the individual mind; there is no objective truth that exists apart from each individual, or if there is, it cannot be known. There would seem to be a contradiction in claiming that we can objectively know that there is no objective truth. *Cynicism* allows for some objective truth, but its adherents claim that the meaning of life is all subjective and this is why people defend their incompatible beliefs with no resolution. Interestingly, however, we tend *not* to debate matters that we believe to be subjective (e.g., a person has a toothache), and certainly the difficulty in coming to agreement on a matter does not in itself suggest that no agreement is possible.

Nihilists insist that life is meaningless, so that even subjective beliefs have no value. They are unable to establish criteria by which truth can be known. Their dilemma helps us realize that there is an intuitive dimension to discerning what is or is not truth. *Naturalists* insist that matter and energy are all that exist in the world, but cannot explain how thoughts about matter and energy have any value.

Moral Relativists claim there is no objective right and wrong and point to the diversity of ethical belief systems as evidence. However, it is striking how much similarity there is across various moralities; not only is it almost impossible to coexist with others without insisting on some kind of common ground from which we appeal for perceived moral violations, but it appears that human beings disagree more on the application of moral values than they do on the basics (see more on this in ch. 9). *Pantheists* have difficulty explaining all the diversity, including violence and inconsistent moral practice, in our universe that is by their claim unified.

Monotheists propose that a holy, intelligent, and powerful deity is the source of all that exists, and most easily accounts for human ability to know what is true and discern what is good. Its claims are rooted in testimony that God has acted and spoken to and among human beings. The monotheistic worldviews have their own challenges, notably the presence of evil and suffering in a world overseen by a powerful and presumably benevolent divine being. What is called *Postmodernism* is basically the loss of the Naturalist's confidence in the ability of the human mind to discern truth (similar to *Skepticism*) while still holding out hope that human beings may eventually figure it out. *Pluralism* is common in our current cultural climate, seeking to draw upon valuable insights from other worldviews. In the end, it is one more claim to know what is true while rejecting what others claim to be true.

Which Lens Is the Best?
At this point you may be wondering whether it is possible to determine whether one worldview is superior to another. Or are we like the goldfish in the fishbowl? Because it swims in water and has no alternate experience, it has no way of identifying the nature of its environment. If that is the case with us, we are simply trapped within the worldview environment we have been given at the outset of our lives.

Perhaps another illustration can help. A series of seemingly random black dots is evident on a light background. Our attempt to make sense of our experiences can be likened to connecting the dots into a pattern. But we then realize that it is possible to connect the dots in more than one way that takes all the dots into account, and that others have done so:

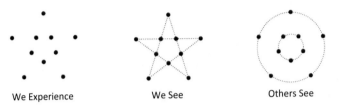

We Experience   We See   Others See

If this summarizes the nature of our situation, there is no way to prefer one way of connecting the dots to another. But suppose we commit to the first pattern and then discover additional considerations that fit only within the second pattern:

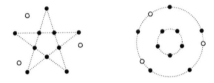

In this case, we may have a basis upon which to prefer the second pattern, and a different worldview, over the first. We might also contemplate whether we have the courage to change worldviews if such new information comes to our attention.

Worldviews and Your Job

We might seem to be moving away from our expressed intent to identify a fitting job or profession. Consider that if ours is indeed a life of adventure, part of it must be to consider how we can know anything at all. Otherwise, how are we to identify something as specific as one's calling? But consider also that worldviews, because they are like glasses through which we see the world, affect how we perceive a job or a profession. As you read the descriptions of four perspectives on work below, ask which of these are implications of a particular worldview and, if so, which worldview.

1. *Staying Alive.* For many persons, job choice is not an option. They must take whatever is available and make the most of it. Sometimes this is desperate and demeaning; other times, it is simply undesirable, either because of the salary or working conditions, or because the job or profession does not match well with a person's gifts and passions. Those in this situation sometime merely tolerate the job; some look for ways to care for others, whether coworkers or customers.

2. *Live for the Weekend.* Some people choose a job because it is the least distasteful or because the pay is good, all with the purpose of getting away from the job as soon as possible where the fun and fulfillment are actually found (the "weekend").

3. *My Empire.* For others, work is a means of self-fulfillment, using the job as a way to control others, to control the world, or to achieve other personal goals. This approach is much more likely than the previous to result in high dedication and diligence in the workplace, for obvious reasons. In the happier cases, it involves a sense of satisfaction in the immediate outcome of the job itself, such as the product achieved or the service accomplished. This satisfaction, however, is focused more on the one working than it is on those who pay for and receive the service or product.

4. *Work Addiction.* The fourth way to engage work is by obsession. Some people are committed to work largely for its own sake. They cannot stop working, even when it is not required for financial reasons, and even when it hinders them from healthy family and other personal relationships.

5. *Service.* The final major approach pays attention to the product or service involved with the job or profession. This does *not* mean neglecting the importance of earning an income and the enjoyment of accomplishing something of personal satisfaction. However, in the course of their job, those taking this approach are concerned to accomplish a benefit for other people and not just for themselves.

The issue of worldviews and how they affect our attitude toward work will be taken up again later. We will in addition distinguish between job and vocation. For now, we turn to a different topic: an examination of how to understand our identity. In the process, we will also consider some harmful traps to avoid.

Questions for Reflection and Discussion
1. Which worldview do you think is most likely your own? What indicators lead you to that conclusion?
2. Are some worldviews better than others? How would you know?
3. Is a narrative or a propositional way of explaining a worldview more helpful to you?
4. Are you open to allowing your own worldview to be evaluated for health and accuracy? Why or why not?
5. Of the four approaches to work described, which have you observed in the workplace or elsewhere?

Suggestions for Further Reading
Peter Kreeft, *The Journey: A Spiritual Roadmap for Modern Pilgrims.* Downers Grove, IL: InterVarsity, 1996.
James W. Sire, *Naming the Elephant: Worldview as a Concept,* 2nd ed. Downers Grove, IL: InterVarsity, 2015.
_____, *The Universe Next Door: A Basic Worldview Catalog,* 5th ed. Downers Grove, IL: InterVarsity, 2009.
Brian J. Walsh and J. Richard Middleton, *The Transforming Vision: Shaping a Christian Worldview.* Downers Grove, IL: InterVarsity, 1984.
Steve Wilkens and Mark L. Sanford, *Hidden Worldviews: Eight Cultural Stories that Shape Our Lives.* Downers Grove, IL: InterVarsity, 2009.

CHAPTER 3

Identity and Call

Some people love their jobs, but even the best jobs have times, situations, and relationships that can cause frustration. Some of these are displayed dramatically in two films from the late 1990s: *Office Space* and *Clockwatchers*. In the first, Peter Gibbons (Ron Livingston) is a computer engineer who hates his job at Initech. Little things are annoying (the receptionist who repeatedly answers the phone with a cheerful "Just a moment!" and the sound of Milton's radio), but company processes are especially vexing: triple reminders to put a cover on the TPS reports, condescending bosses Bill, Bob, and Bob, the decision to downsize workers. We learn that all this might be tolerable if only Peter was doing something that meant anything to him.

The job complications of temp workers are explored in *Clockwatchers*. Iris (Toni Collette) is a shy, insecure young woman who can never land a permanent job and cannot believe her father's encouraging words that she is really talented. At her latest short-term position, she and three other women, equally isolated from the permanent employees, find camaraderie in their mutual circumstances. Though Iris works hard and hopes for the best, she eventually learns that once again she has not made the cut to be full-time.

Crises of the Work World

Despite affluence compared to the rest of the world, living in Western culture means dealing with crises related to work.[9] For some, there is a crisis simply of *employment*. They graduate from college or some other form of training and find that the jobs of their expertise and interest have few openings as compared to number of applicants. Or during employment, their positions are eliminated for any number of reasons. Within the job world, there is often a crisis of *confidence*. A person can experience failure, setback, and/or disappointment. There may be criticism or lack of affirmation. One's profession can change making it difficult to keep appropriately informed or trained. Ideals, plans, and hopes seem more easily dashed than ever.

A third crisis involves *focus*. Ours is a distracted society, not least due to our technology. We operate in an environment filled with advertisements and other siren songs trying to pull us away from our present concern. Voices compete with each other for our imaginations and for priority on our values ladder. When we try to get away for a weekend or even a well-deserved vacation, the technology goes along, buzzing and jingling at us so that we can never truly rest and recharge.

But by far the most tragic crisis among us is the crisis of *purpose* experienced by the employees in *Office Space* and *Clockwatchers*. Behind the question of work is the bigger question of what life is all about. Some have claimed that contemporary Western culture is the first in the history of the world that does not know why it is here. Certainly there are people within this culture who claim to know, but there is little consensus about a larger purpose. The Roman Empire, for example, though its populace embraced various understandings of purpose, imposed an official cultural ideology. But in our day any such understanding has fragmented.

So, on the whole, we live our lives not knowing what our existence is about or how we should fit into it. Of course, this is precisely the issue being addressed by this book. The concept of vocation cannot, by itself, make sure you get hired in the field of your interest and training; it can only indirectly address the challenges to confidence that may come your way;

and it cannot increase your focus on the tasks at hand. However, it can help you with the most important crisis, the crisis of meaning. We turn now to consider some traps that lead to an inadequate sense of identity, and thus a false sense of meaning or purpose.

Seven Traps We Can Avoid

Gordon Smith argues that thinking vocationally comes with distinct advantages.[10] The following list is inspired by his suggestions, framed in terms of "traps" that can be avoided by living one's life with a vocation mindset. A trap is something deceptive that moves us away from a truly healthy and meaningful life. Note the statements of personal identity associated with each trap.

- I am the center of all, and everything revolves around me.
  The trap of dysfunctional self-absorption
- I am what people think of me.
  The trap of needing to please everyone
- I am what I own.
  The trap of consumerism
- I am what I do or produce.
  The trap of the tyranny of time
- I am valuable only if I'm better than someone else.
  The trap of comparison with others
- I am valuable only if I can reach impossible goals.
  The trap of artificial standards of excellence
- I do not have the abilities I need to succeed.
  The trap of pretense and the fear of accountability

No doubt many of the items on this list are very familiar. These traps distort our relationships with others, both on and off the job. Vocation, by helping us avoid these traps, has the potential to help us be content with who we are and who we have been created to become.

It may seem like this vocation idea promises a lot, but that is because our ability to find satisfaction in life depends very much on how we understand ourselves and what we think we are supposed to be doing here. "Understanding ourselves" can also be described as "identity." Significantly, these traps have a connection with a person's sense of who they are. In order to embrace a healthy idea of who I am, I will need to reject a lot of false options that tend to be passed around in contemporary Western cultures. Everything from advertisements to the rationale given for choosing one's job or profession is loaded with messages about identity. These messages are then reinforced by people we live and work with who are buying into those messages. In order to set such false markers aside, we need to find and embrace more positive ones.[11]

A Story about a Business

Jesus told a variety of stories to help us understand better who God is, who we are, and what God is up to in the world. Each of these stories is fairly simple, but the reason Jesus told so many with so much variety is because the issues addressed can become very complex. One of the most important of these stories goes like this (Matt. 25:14-30, loosely paraphrased):

> A business owner decided to go on a journey. So he called his employees together and entrusted his assets to them, each according to his ability. To one he gave $50,000, to another $20,000, and to a third $10,000. The first two put their boss's money to work and doubled what they had been given, but the third employee hid the money in a hole in the ground. The owner eventually returned and settled accounts. He was really happy with the first two. "Well done! You've made me very pleased!" he exclaimed, and then gave them a promotion and responsibility for additional matters. The third employee explained that he knew the boss to be harsh, reaping and gathering where he had not planted, so out of fear he hid the money and now returned it. The boss declared that third employee to be wicked and lazy. He asked why he didn't at least invest the money in the bank. He then took the $10,000 and gave it to the first employee. Jesus explains: "For to all those who have, more will be given, and they will have an abundance; but from those who produce nothing, even what they have will be taken away." The owner fired that worthless employee who went out weeping and wailing with regret.

This parable gives an interesting window into the work world. It reflects both the challenge and the opportunities of life on the job. In addition, because Jesus used this story to teach about the project called "God's kingdom," it gives us some ideas about what God expects as we live out the call that is on our lives. Jesus asks us to think about aspects of our relationship with God in terms of this story, as servants to whom God gives certain tasks.

The owner provided *opportunities* for his employees to share in the work. The level of responsibility with which they were entrusted was based upon their *abilities*, none the same as the other. To accomplish their tasks they were given *resources* in the form of money, though our resources could include education and training, our experience, and much more. These three together—opportunity, ability, and resources—made up their *mission*.

Likewise each of us, separately and in connection with others, is given a mission to carry out, and for this we will be held accountable. The parable invites us to reflect on its three main elements: the opportunities before us, the abilities we have, and the resources we have been given. But lest we find this to be heavy news, notice how much joy and celebration there is for those who do their part!

The story also illustrates one form of failure: the third employee was so afraid of the owner that he failed to do anything of value. We might also productively reflect on this story in regard to the identity traps mentioned previously. For example, imagine one of the owner's employees deciding, when he came to work, that he was more important than the boss. What if one of the employees became concerned about pleasing someone else or some other group more than pleasing the owner. Suppose one of the employees decided that getting paid and buying things were more important than helping make the boss successful. How might things change if employees became so production focused that they assumed the owner had no concern for the employees' health, well-being, or enjoyment of life.

What if the employees started competing with one another or became jealous rather than simply being faithful with the resources and abilities they were given. Or what if the employees refused to believe that the owner was really pleased when he said, "Well done," and insisted on exhausting themselves to produce more. Suppose one of the employees decided to pretend he had more resources and more abilities than he really had, and because of being ashamed of what he actually was given, was unable to accomplish what concerned the owner most.

Bible Identity Markers

If we are to avoid these traps, we will need to think of who we *are* and not only about what we *do*. Here and elsewhere the Bible offers us that possibility. That is, the Bible offers us identity markers, many of which are just the antidote for the traps listed at the beginning of this chapter. Here are some of them, based on the Matthew 25 story, and worded to counter the dysfunctional statements in that previous list.

- I am a servant working for project goals larger than myself.
  Freed from dysfunctional self-absorption
- I am accountable to one boss.
  Freed from needing to please everyone
- I have an employer prosperous enough to care for my needs.
  Freed from consumerism
- I am adequately resourced for my mission.
  Freed from the tyranny of time
- I am a complementary employee of the boss's team.
  Freed from comparison with others
- I have a boss who has reasonable assignments for me.
  Freed from artificial standards of excellence
- I have the abilities to accomplish what is expected of me.
  Freed from pretense and the fear of accountability

Here are a few more Bible identity markers:

- I am a child and God is my loving parent (Matt. 6:5-15).
- I am a sheep and Jesus is the shepherd who cares for my needs (John 10:11).
- I am the salt of the earth, light of the world (Matt. 5:13-14).
- I am a citizen of God's kingdom (Phil. 3:20).
- I am a brick in God's temple (Eph. 2:21).
- I am a branch connected to Jesus, the Vine, and to God's people (John 15:1-11).

These are stated in individual terms, but part of our challenge in the West is to recognize how much we also need to think in terms of groups. Try reading over the lists above in the plural to see how that affects your thinking about identity, e.g., *we are* adequately resourced for *our* mission.

If we remind ourselves of true statements about our identity and practice them, we are less likely to fall into identity traps. This is because the identity statements we find in the Bible assume the basics that underlie the concept of vocation, such as, God made us and loves us, my life belongs to God, God is in charge, I am accountable for living out the life that God has called me/us to, and Jesus is our model.

Three Callings

When we put the idea of God assigning tasks to people in the context of other teachings in the Bible (to be discussed in more detail later), it is helpful to think about *three* callings.[12] The *primary calling* is the call to a reconciled relationship with our Creator, to salvation, to knowing God and being known by God. It is connected to the call to repentance (changing our direction) in the ministries of John the Baptist and Jesus (Matt. 3:2; 4:17). This call arises from the brokenness of human beings; it is the beginning of making that brokenness whole again; and very importantly it includes becoming part of God's community. All people are called in this way, and each of us must be sure we have answered that call.

The *secondary calling*, also known as *vocation*, is the call to mission, to being a significant part of God's work in the world, to a meaningful living out of one's life by making the world a better place. This calling is the main focus of this book.

Finally, there is the *immediate calling*, which means putting the first two callings into action, the tasks of the day. These are the things that take priority at any given time, including our anticipated agenda, but also matters not directly connected to our vocation: spilled milk, flat tires, supporting a friend or neighbor in a crisis, power outages, or opening a door for someone on crutches. The immediate calling is one we all know about because each day we face a sequence of things to which we must attend. And surprises happen no matter how well our day is planned. Addressing the unexpected, including crises of whatever magnitude, is a part of living in this world, and it often is part of caring for those around us. This third category helps us to distinguish other urgent matters from those that are more specifically part of our vocation.

To summarize, God calls people in three ways: to a relationship with their Creator and to God's people, to a mission, and to a world of daily tasks with surprises.

A Process for Discerning Your Vocation

A sense of call or purpose can come in a variety of ways. However, some of the approaches people use to discern this direction have had mixed results. Some people take a personality or aptitude test and assume that will point them in the right direction. While helpful (see below), this information alone may not be enough. Some borrow Gideon's use of a sign (see Judg. 6). Gideon was trying to decide if God was really going to help him, so he proposed a test with the condition that if the fleece was wet and the ground was dry, he could rely on God. Similarly, some people decide that if a particular event happens (or doesn't happen)—if they are offered a certain job, if a friend calls before noon on a certain day—they will take that event as a sign of God's plans for their life. Another approach is to pray and wait (and often wait . . . and wait . . .) to get some kind of a vision or dramatic experience. While this has been known to happen, God does not seem to work that way with everyone. However, God *does* want to make each person's calling known to them.

So how can a person discover their calling? While there is no simple answer to that question, and no guaranteed formula, there are some time-tested ways that people have used to get clarity in this area. In describing these exercises, it is important to emphasize that they must be used as creatively as possible to allow for the uniqueness of each person. What worked well for someone else may not work so well for you, and vice versa. It is also helpful to focus not so much on the whole rest of your life, but instead to seek what might be the best next step for you. This is true whether you are in college, thinking about choosing a major that could lead to a specific profession, or a person making a midlife adjustment, thinking about possibly changing jobs or professions, or someone of almost any age thinking about cross-cultural mission work or some other voluntary commitment of service.

We should start with a simple question: Am I willing to do what seems to be the right or best thing? Or, if embracing a Christian worldview, Am I willing to do what God wants me to do? If your answer to such questions is "No," the process described here could lead to more frustration than clarity. But if the answer is truly "Yes," and it may take a while to fully commit to that "Yes," then these can be helpful.

The ideas below borrow in part from a process used by Quaker Christians called "listening for clearness." Clarity of God's direction can come to us through three venues, introduced briefly here and followed by further explanation:

(1) Through **our own lives**. Quaker author Parker Palmer encourages us "to listen to what our lives are saying *and* take notes on it, lest we forget our own truth or deny that we ever heard it."[13]
(2) Through the **Scriptures and other texts**. These can give us clues to our own gifts and calling.
(3) Through the **lives of others**. Good ideas come from other people, and you may discern God speaking to you in this way. This can happen either directly or when someone lives in a way that inspires us to emulate. It is also important to test the ideas we get from items 1 and 2 above with friends and those who are wise.

One • Our Own Lives: What Is Your SHAPE?

Because acronyms are fascinating things, we are going to use one here to help organize the *first venue* of the process mentioned above, listening through our own lives.[14] As we read in Ephesians 2:10, " For we are God's handiwork, created in Christ Jesus to do good works, which God prepared in advance for us to do." Thus, each person is uniquely crafted to do certain things, though the involvements of life, including tragedies of various types, intersect with God's goals for our lives. But, as you may find, sometimes such events lead to an amazing combination of gifts and experience that can motivate us to powerful forms of service. For this venue, think and reflect prayerfully about each of the following items whose first letters spell SHAPE. (For a further explanation of each item, see Appendix A).

Successes and Struggles: Projects and experiences that went well; failures, hardships, and broken places.
Heart: Your passions, the things that get you emotionally energized. Consider especially (a) the needs of other people, and (b) specific hopes and "dreams" — things in your imagination.
Abilities: Your so-called "natural" talents and skills; also spiritual gifts mentioned in the Bible.
Personality: The complex of behavioral preferences and emotional orientations that characterize you.
Experience: Any other aspects of your experience and background.

Such a review of your life may take courage, but all these SHAPE elements can provide clues to your life purpose.

Two • Scripture and Other Texts

The *second venue* is to reflect intentionally on portions of the Bible or other special sources. This can take several forms, some likely more significant for you than others. One way to get started is to consider whether there are certain stories, poems, or films that you already know are especially important to you, that "stick" with you because they are exciting in a deep sort of way. Perhaps they are trying to tell you something. A second kind of engagement is to consider sections of the Bible that are focused on God's call on people's lives. Here are some of those: Genesis 32:22-32; Exodus 31:1-6; 1 Samuel 3:2-9; Matthew 5:1-16; Luke 19:1-10; John 1:35-50; Romans 12:1-8; 1 Corinthians 10:31; Galatians 5:22-23; Ephesians 4:7-13; Colossians 3:23-24. Think about other parts of the Bible that are especially important to you and review them as well.

Before moving on to the third venue, reflect a bit on what you notice in the first and second venues. Ask whether there are any common threads that run through some or all of the elements. For example, do you find yourself concerned about persons who live in conditions of poverty? Do you have some natural aptitudes toward organization or motivating others? Do you have an outgoing personality? Have you had experiences that give you confidence with some dimension of helping the poor? Obviously, persons of a variety of personalities, abilities, and experience could address poverty in meaningful ways. But do you see your combination fitting together and pointing in a certain direction?

Three • **The Lives of Others**

After completing the above, it is time for the *third venue.* This step is where you can reflect on someone who has been a model for you. Even more it concerns taking counsel with those who know you well and care about you. Inform them what you have discovered so far and what you are thinking. Ask them for some responses. Do your ideas align with what they know about you? Do they see some complications you haven't thought about? Are there some factors that make this an even better fit than you have realized so far? Those who are part of a Christian community may have a structure in place for discernment of various kinds and should consider seeking out support and affirmation within that group.

An alternate way to accomplish the third venue is called the "clearness committee." A Quaker practice is to arrange for a group of people to ask a person (you, in this case) questions about his or her goals and values. If you gather such a group, begin by recounting what you have identified in venues one and two previously. Then, the persons should start asking questions for you to consider, but they should give no advice. The person receiving the questions can clarify various points and respond if he or she wishes to do so. However, the person need not answer the questions.

A Mission Statement

So, what to do with the results of your exploration? Christine and Tom Sine, in their helpful book on vocation, suggest that Christians should articulate a sense of purpose for their lives every bit as much as businesses and other groups do. Such a concise expression of your sense of purpose can be called a "mission statement" that states what you believe to be your calling (vocation).[15] This is what you believe to be the case, as you best understand it, for right now. It could change in the future, or at least you might find dimensions of it that you have not thought about now. For a Christian, this is a statement about your role in God's kingdom work on earth, the way you will put feet to the prayer, "your kingdom come, your will be done, on earth as it is in heaven!" (Matt. 6:10).

Here are two examples. Jody loves people and likes to be with a group. She gets satisfaction out of seeing children improve in school and has majored in education. Her statement could read like this: *My mission is to use my education, my abilities, and my interest in people to educate children so that they can learn about their world and participate fully in it.*

David is a businessman who seeks to care for creation and particularly for people who have been excluded from the workplace by their disabilities. He found that disabled people make great employees and were highly motivated. His statement could be something like this: *My mission is to restore excluded lives by employing disabled people, and to care for creation through a business that recycles waste materials.*

Having a mission statement helps us focus our lives in terms of our relationships with friends, family, people on the job, and the folks we go to church with. It helps us with important life choices, including how we use our time and money, where we live (both part of the world and specific neigh-borhood), what profession and job we take, and even whom we might marry. Regarding the material in this chapter, it is a way to put the suggested process into action and see what you find. (For some additional information concerning the mission statement process, see Appendix A.)

We turn now to consider an essential aspect of relating to people and things we encounter in our world.

Questions for Reflection and Discussion

1.   How do you answer the question, "Who am I?" Do any of the identity markers presented in this chapter look helpful for answering that question? If so, which?
2.   Consider Jesus' parable of the business owner. Do you find yourself more like the first employees or the third? Why?
3.   Do you find yourself in any of the traps listed in this chapter? What would make it easier to avoid them?
4.   Explain the three "callings." In what ways is it helpful to think in these three categories?
5.   Examine each item in the SHAPE acronym. List one thing true about yourself for each letter.
6.   What do you think about the process suggested for discerning your calling? Do you think this could help you personally?

Suggestions for Further Reading

Richard T. Hughs, *Myths America Lives By*. Urbana and Chicago: University of Illinois Press, 2004.

Timothy Keller and Katherine Leary Alsdorf, *Every Good Endeavor: Connecting Your Work to God's Work*. New York: Riverhead, 2012.

George Lakoff and Mark Johnson, *Metaphors We Live By*, 2nd ed. Chicago: University of Chicago Press, 2003.

Parker Palmer, *Let Your Life Speak*. San Francisco, CA: Jossey-Bass, 2000.

Christine and Tom Sine, *Living on Purpose: Finding God's Best for Your Life*. Grand Rapids, MI: Baker, 2002.

CHAPTER 4

Invitation to Faith

As a young boy, I loved adventure. I wanted to climb things, build forts, and hang my feet over ledges with hundreds of feet of nothing below me. One representative incident happened when my family was having a picnic in a place called Papago Park in the greater Phoenix area. It was an easy climb to get to the "Hole in the Rock," which called to me irresistibly. But it was a bit more of a challenge for a boy of nine to climb further up on top of the massive rock formation. Nevertheless, I got in line with some people who were walking carefully along a ledge that eventually led to the top.

About halfway there I got stuck. I pressed myself against the rock, my feet on the narrow path, but I was afraid to go either forward or backward. So I took a peek over my shoulder at the fifty-foot drop that seemed to be my destiny. As I did so, my young life actually flashed before my eyes, like an old slide show of still pictures—me and my cousins, me and my family, me and my dog. I knew I was going to die.

Just then, however, a man I had never met, coming in line behind me and seeing my predicament, asked if I needed help. I certainly did! But could I trust him? I didn't know much about him, but I rapidly sized him up. He seemed friendly enough and strong enough. Then he made a proposal, which let me know he was wise enough. "Here," he said, "let me put my hand on your back. I'll hold you up while you keep going."

I placed my faith in this man, cooperated with his instructions, and it worked! I then easily scampered to the top of the rock, and lived to tell the tale.

The purpose of this chapter is to consider how normal and how big a part of our lives is the simple matter of relying on other people and other things. In the process, I will also describe faith as it is presented in the Bible and what it means to have faith in something ultimate. The word *faith* is one of those religious-sounding terms that most of us partly understand. It has something to do with confidence in, or commitment to, someone or something. But the word can be used with several meanings. Sometimes we use the term in a general way to indicate loyalty, such as, "She maintains her faith in General Motors regardless what others say." At other times the word is used for belief in something for which there is no proof or in the face of conflicting evidence, such as, "He has faith in his coach despite the team's poor record in past years." Sometimes by *faith* we mean a particular religious system or perspective, like "the Christian faith" or "the Jewish faith."

Whether or not we use the term *faith*, we all practice some form of it on a regular basis. As in my rock climbing, we *take risks* by *placing confidence in something or someone* even though there is no way we can be completely sure what the result will be. In fact, it is probably impossible to go a single day without exercising faith to some extent. When someone orders an item over the phone or on the Internet, she has faith that the person or company will actually send that item, and has faith in the shipment service that is hired to deliver it. When you loan a friend your car keys, you are exercising faith that the person will treat your car well. Cases such as these demonstrate that faith—taking the risk to rely on a particular person or object— is a regular part of human living.

When we talk about faith in a religious dimension, then, we are not talking about something unique or unusual to the human condition. We are simply discussing how this normal experience applies to something of greatest importance, or "ultimate concern" (theologian Paul Tillich's term). For Christians, that object of greatest importance is the God described in the Bible as the Creator of the universe. It is also applied to God's son, Jesus Christ, the Messiah, who came to earth and called people to join God's kingdom. As indicated above, the term *faith* can also refer to a set of beliefs, a "faith system." But for Christians, this begins with confidence in a God who is personal.

The Bible's Words for Faith

Though it is illustrated throughout, most of the Bible's instruction about faith is found in the New Testament. One of the complications in reading and understanding what the Bible says on this issue is that the English language uses a variety of terms to express the concept. The Greek language of the New Testament most often uses a set of words that are similar in their Greek spelling: a verb (*pisteuo*), a noun (*pistis*), and an adjective (*pistos*). In English, these are often translated "to believe," "faith," and "faithful" respectively. Notice that there is a Greek verb for faith, but English does not use the term *faith* as a verb; the closest we come to expressing faith as an *action* is when we say that someone "has faith" or "believes." A familiar Bible verse is typically translated this way, "For God so loved the world that he gave his one and only son, that whoever believes in him shall not perish but have eternal life" (John 3:16). Instead of the word *believes*, we could also translate the Greek phrase like this: "whoever *exercises faith* in him." The verb (action word) means to do something, in this case, to risk confidence in someone or something in a way that affects one's life and decisions. In order to pay attention to the verb for faith, we will need to watch for the word *believe* in our Bibles.

The *objects* of faith in the New Testament are primarily Jesus Christ and the good news (gospel) associated with him. We are invited to have faith in him, to believe in him, and thus to be saved. Wholehearted confidence in Jesus is a way of describing the right way to be in relationship with him. It is important, then, to appreciate Jesus' mission and plan as the context for this faith. Jesus called people to "Repent for the kingdom of heaven has come near" (Matt. 4:17). He described the citizens of the kingdom, taught about the character of the kingdom, and urged people to follow him to become part of the kingdom. Whatever we propose about faith in Jesus must be consistent with his mission to invite people to join this divine community lived out on earth today.

Christian Descriptions of Faith

From the beginning, Christians have described faith from a variety of angles. Note these examples:

- Now faith is confidence in what we hope for and assurance about what we do not see. (Heb. 11:1)
- For we maintain that a person is justified by faith apart from the works of the law. (Rom. 3:28)
- You see that a person is considered righteous by what they do and not by faith alone. (James 2:24)

Sometimes these statements have seemed in tension with one another. Martin Luther in the sixteenth century was convinced that the Apostle Paul's understanding of faith as being independent of the law (Rom. 3:28 above) was a breakthrough that corrected an Old Testament approach to salvation based on work approved by God. On the other hand, because the book of James says that human activity *is* important to God, Luther thought this book should be removed from the New Testament.

We may wonder whether James really disagreed with Paul, reflecting differences among Christians even in the first century, or whether he might be correcting a misunderstanding or distortion of the kind of statements made by Paul. Even today Christians sometime debate whether "faith alone" is enough for salvation or whether "faith plus works" is what the Bible teaches. We will return to this issue below.

Three Historical Approaches to Faith

Let's take a brief tour of three major ways Christians have approached faith. The first comes in two forms that are concerned with the *mental content of faith*. Some of the church leaders in the early centuries after Christ took an illuminist position, that faith was a gift of God that illumined the human mind so that people could believe the truth.[16] They receive an ability to see things that equip them to choose correctly. A scholastic perspective likewise supposed that true faith is a mental agreement concerning the truth of certain statements, e.g., about God, Jesus, and other matters presented in Christian teaching. Together these theories may be called "intellectual" approaches.

This concept of faith recognizes that there is an important intellectual element to embracing what is true. However, such an approach may be challenged on the grounds that it focuses narrowly on the mind rather than considering the whole person. Also, such views may partner with a nonbiblical dualism between mind and body, celebrating the former as superior and devaluing the latter as somehow evil or inferior.[17]

A second approach is called "fiducial" after the Latin term for faith, *fides*. The emphasis in this approach is *reliance upon God*. The intellectual approach focuses on what God has said and done in the past, while the fiducial approach focuses on the future, a trust and hope that God will make all things work out for good. Those who advocate this understanding of faith, such as Martin Luther, tend to emphasize the individual and his or her relationship with God. The strength of this theory is the intimacy it promotes between a person and God, and its confidence in the ability of God to deliver the person from their difficulties. It is a reaction against the potential coldness of intellectual theories and against any approach to faith that stresses the necessity of human action as part of salvation. Proponents of this approach minimize the importance of the mind and often insist that, while good actions follow genuine faith, faith itself does not include actions.

However, by devaluing the mind somewhat and actions even more, the fiducial approach also fails to embrace the whole person. Diminishing the mind can result in an emotionalism that is shallow in content, and loss of concern for action can lead to suspicion that obedience is an attempt to earn one's salvation. Dietrich Bonhoeffer labeled the latter problem "cheap grace" for relying on Christ to do everything. It does not allow for Jesus' strong emphasis on discipleship and following his instructions. This approach also seems at odds with the Old Testament prophets and John the Baptist, who called people to repent and to practice a righteous lifestyle.[18]

Finally, a third approach to faith is called "performative." This approach does not necessarily reject what is provided by the intellectual and fiducial theories, but it emphasizes that *obedient action* is a part of faith, not something that may simply follow or be an optional aspect of genuine faith. This has sometimes been advocated by liberation theologians and others as a corrective to both an emphasis on the mind and an individualistic emphasis upon trust. The performative approach, however, is sometimes overly connected with political agenda and risks the message that salvation must be earned by what one does.[19]

We will now consider how employing the strengths of all three of these historic approaches—intellectual, fiducial, and performative—might help us appreciate a fresh understanding of faith.

A Parable

The three theories described above each offer an aspect of biblical faith that is indispensable. And each approach, if taken in isolation, results in a distortion that has harmful consequences. The following illustration may help. Let's say that a man is sick and seriously hurting. He wants to get better, so he considers going to a local doctor. If he places his *faith* in the doctor, this faith will involve three important elements.

First, he must be convinced in his *mind* that this person really is a credible medical physician and is qualified to treat his illness. For example, he may confirm that his friends testify to positive experiences with the doctor, and may check to see that the person did indeed graduate from a credentialed medical school and has a license to practice in his state.

Second, he will *trust* what the doctor has to offer him. This could mean setting aside his own ideas of what it would take to make himself better, and choosing the doctor's assessment instead of what he might read on the Internet. Finally, he will need to follow the doctor's instructions, which usually means *doing* or *not* doing something, such as taking a prescription or avoiding certain foods.

The point of this story is not that a person who goes to a doctor should accept everything the doctor says or never get a second opinion. This tale is designed to illustrate faith; to the extent that the man in the story has faith in the doctor, he will engage all three elements: thinking, trusting, and doing. If all three elements are not involved, there is a distortion of faith, or a weak or even a false faith. For example, if the man had no reason to believe the doctor was qualified to practice medicine, but mindlessly trusted and took the prescriptions anyway, we would call him gullible rather than practicing genuine faith.

If the man took the medicine prescribed by the doctor, but kept searching medical journals and Internet sites, and also made appointments with other doctors for their advice, we would think the man mistrusted either the doctor's competence (Was his diploma genuine?) or good intentions (Could the doctor be making money from prescription sales?). We might also wonder about other possible motives for taking the medicine (Was it to get his wife to stop nagging him?).

Finally, if the man bought the prescribed medicine but never took it, we would also question whether he really had confidence in the doctor's plan to help him get well.

Simply stated, true faith in the doctor means (1) knowing why the doctor should be trusted, (2) trusting the doctor's competence and good intentions rather than someone else's, and (3) doing what the doctor says.

Three Indispensable Aspects of Faith

We may now consider how the Bible addresses each of the faith elements.[20] First, there is an important *intellectual* dimension to faith:

> Jesus and his disciples went on to the villages around Caesarea Philippi. On the way he asked them, "Who do people say I am?" [28] They replied, "Some say John the Baptist; others say Elijah; and still others, one of the prophets." [29] "But what about you?" he asked. "Who do you say I am?" Peter answered, "You are the Messiah." (Mark 8:27-29)

Jesus said to [Martha], "I am the resurrection and the life. The one who believes in me will live, even though they die; [26] and whoever lives by believing in me will never die. Do you believe this?" [27] "Yes, Lord," she replied, "I believe that you are the Messiah, the Son of God, who is to come into the world." (John 11:25-27)

But these [stories of Jesus' miracles] are written that you may believe that Jesus is the Messiah, the Son of God, and that by believing you may have life in his name. (John 20:31)

Christianity makes certain historical, moral, and cognitive claims and proposes them to people as a way of making sense of their lives. When Christians live their life of faith, part of it involves a firm conviction about the essential beliefs that the Bible teaches, including those about Jesus Christ.

To avoid the danger of scholasticism, it is important to take an illuminist approach to the intellectual aspect of faith. It helps remind us that salvation is always a gift of God's grace, and is reflected when we hear people of faith say something like, "Once I was blind, but now I can see." The person is able to recognize that certain things are true and to believe those things. We should note that this belief is based upon evidence, just as a person's willingness to have faith in a doctor is based on certain kinds of evidence. Yet Thomas Groome cautions, "Christian faith is at least belief, but it must also be more than belief if it is to be a lived reality."[21]

Second, there is an important *trust* dimension to Christian faith. This concerns the *motive* for what a person does. For Christianity, this dimension takes the form of a relationship of trust and confidence in a personal God who saves through Jesus Christ. Believers express their trust by means of loyalty, love, and attachment to this God. Because God is faithful, we confidently reject other forms of security, such as other saviors and even our own work. It is the redemptive work of Christ that saves us:

For it is by grace you have been saved, through faith—and this is not from yourselves, it is the gift of God— [9] not by works, so that no one can boast. (Eph. 2:8-9)

Realization of God's power, our dependence upon that power, and God's faithfulness to us can lead to trust, awe, wonder, reverence, adoration, gratitude, and petition on our part. Our confidence in God leads us to realize and remember that the kingdom is a blessing, and it has already come in Jesus Christ. Salvation has been won for us. There is a caution, though; the dark side of trust is presumption, to insist on certain outcomes or actions of God. Genuine trust does not demand a specific plan, but relies on God's wisdom.

For these reasons we can live our lives with joy, peace, and happiness. Jesus came that we might have life and have it abundantly (John 10:10). He came that his joy might be in us and that our joy might be complete (John 15:11).[22]

Finally, faith involves *performance* or doing. The will of God must be done by loving God and loving one's neighbor as oneself (Matt. 22:37-38). God is in the process of creating new people who can live this way. The verse that follows Ephesians 2:8-9 about being saved by grace (v. 10, quoted below) reads,

> For we are God's handiwork, created in Christ Jesus to do good works, which God prepared in advance for us to do. (Eph. 2:10)

The Apostle Paul understood that faith acts itself out. That is why his great letter to the Roman Christians—in which faith and God's grace is so strongly emphasized—begins and concludes with references to the "obedience of faith" (Rom. 1:5; 16:26 NRSV, ESV; see also 15:18). In Groome's words, the faith is *in* the doing, not somehow separate from it. This is why Jesus insisted,

> Not everyone who says to me, "Lord, Lord," will enter the kingdom of heaven, but only the one who does the will of my Father who is in heaven. (Matt. 7:21)

Also,

> For if you forgive other people when they sin against you, your heavenly Father will also forgive you. [15] But if you do not forgive others their sins, your Father will not forgive your sins. (Matt. 6:14-15)

Thus, the call of God on our lives means to *do* things: to engage lovingly with the world, for the sake of the world, so that God's will might be done there. All three faith elements are essential.

Faith Distortions

When we recognize the importance of all three faith elements, it is not surprising that when one or more are devalued, problems arise. Examples of such "faith distortions" are found in the chart below. Each of these five possibilities is addressed several times in the Bible, as the references indicate.

Perhaps it is now evident how Paul and James can seem to be at odds with each other about faith when they actually embrace the same understanding. It is because they are speaking to groups who are in danger of different faith distortions. Paul is speaking to people who need reminding that salvation is a gift, and that their faith must be in God's Messiah. Therefore he emphasizes trust, justification by faith in Jesus in contrast to works of the law (Rom. 3:28). Likewise, his complex teaching about the identity of Jesus and many other topics demonstrates that Paul addressed people's minds as well. Finally, his mission is to accomplish the "obedience of faith," so action is also included (Rom. 1:5; 16:26).

James, on the other hand, spoke to people who needed reminding that faith involves action. So he emphasizes the action aspect of faith in his writing:

> Religion that God our Father accepts as pure and faultless is this: to look after orphans and widows in their distress and to keep oneself from being polluted by the world. (James 1:27)

Yet it is also clear that James understands salvation to be a gift:

> Every good and perfect *gift* is from above, coming down from the Father of the heavenly lights, who does not change like shifting shadows. [18] He chose to *give* us birth through the word of truth, that we might be a kind of firstfruits of all he created. (James 1:17-18, emph. added)

Faith Distortions	Five Dangers	Symptoms
1. Mostly Intellect and Trust, lacking (godly) Action	I T A x x o **Cheap Grace**	We lack a sense of accountability to God and also miss the transformation of our character God is trying to do in us. Matt. 23:2-3; James 2:19; Rom. 12:1-2
2. Mostly Intellect, lacking Trust and Action	I T A x o o **Scholasticism**	We play an academic, often prideful and contentious intellectual game. 1 Cor. 3:18-21; 8:1; 1 John 3:18; 1 Tim. 6:20-21; 2 Tim. 2:23-26
3. Mostly Action, lacking Intellect	I T A o x **Work Addiction**	We become obsessed with work without clear sense of purpose. Disorientation. Eccl. 4:7-8; Matt. 11:28-30; Mark 6:31
4. Mostly Action, lacking Trust	I T A o x **Works Righteousness**	Failing to recognize the extent of our sinfulness, we attempt to earn our salvation by what we do. Fear, pride, manipulation. Rom. 3:21-31; Eph. 2:8-10; Heb. 9:14
5. Mostly Trust, lacking Intellect	I T A o x **Emotionalism**	We operate primarily on feelings and are vulnerable to any new idea coming around. Eph. 4:14; 1 John 2:22-23

This somewhat paradoxical reality of God's involvement with human beings is expressed this way by Paul:

> For God is working in you, giving you the desire and the power to do what pleases him. (Phil. 2:13 NLT)

The good news of the gospel is that God is transforming people to live out the vision for the way God created us in the very beginning. Our reliance upon the God we believe in empowers us to be people of faithful action.

Faith in God

We have been considering how faith in God, as discussed in the Bible, is similar to other experiences we have of faith. When we place our faith in a doctor, in a friend, or in a company, we normally employ all three of the indispensible elements: belief, trust, and action. We do not make the choice of faith without evidence. And it is interesting to note how much the testimony of others contributes to faith, religious or otherwise.[23] But on the other hand, neither do we have definitive proof about whether a doctor will diagnose correctly, or our friend will treat our car with respect.

Note that the three elements are not so much something we must try to "balance." Rather, whenever one element seems to be weak, it indicates that our faith is weak. When we don't follow the doctor's instructions, it is not that we need to prop up the action element of faith in the doctor or trim our knowledge; it indicates our *faith* in the doctor is in poor shape. Growth in faith requires practice: taking risks, learning about faith's object, and acting consistently with what one knows.

And when we consider faith in the God of the Bible, the implications of these factors become much greater. Christianity claims that we must commit ourselves to the One who created us, who is our ultimate Judge, and who died for us showing how much we are loved. If Christianity is correct, our eternal destiny is determined by whether or not we make this commitment. Groome summarizes:

Lived Christian faith has at least three essential activities: believing, trusting, and doing. While they can be distinguished for the sake of clarity, they cannot be separated in the life of the Christian community as if any one of them could exist alone or have priority over the others. Undoubtedly, there are times and circumstances when one dimension will receive more apparent emphasis than the others. And there are individual Christians who by disposition tend to take their life stance more within one dimension or another (for instance, the professional theologian, the contemplative, the social activist). But as a lived reality, the faith life of the community, and to some extent the faith life of every Christian, must include all three activities.[24]

Just how faith in Jesus begins for a person—this commitment to him as Lord—is something of a mystery. It is quite personal and a bit different for each person, as is reflected in believers' testimonies. For those committed to faith in Christ, it is beneficial to recognize the three essential elements, and to make sure that all three are alive and healthy

The Bible describes this life of faith in Jesus in a variety of ways. Here are a few. A Christian is one who *receives the new life that Christ came to give.* Jesus told the Pharisee Nicodemus that he needed to be born again (John 3:7), and Peter praised God who has "given us new birth into a living hope through the resurrection of Jesus Christ from the dead" (1 Pet. 1:3).

A Christian is also one who *joins the story that centers on Jesus.* The plot line of the Bible builds toward Jesus, describes Jesus, then further reflects on Jesus as it goes forward. Part of that story is indicated when Jesus' mother, Mary, was told, "you are to give him the name Jesus, because he will save his people from their sins" (Matt. 1:21).

A third description of a Christian is one who *joins the people or movement of Jesus and obeys what he teaches.* Jesus said, "whoever does not carry their cross and follow me cannot be my disciple" (Luke 14:27).

To sum up, faith in Jesus Christ means repenting—turning away from wrong we are doing, and from other objects of faith—and turning to him, and as a result having our sins forgiven. It means knowing who Jesus is, entrusting ourselves into his care, and doing what he says. It means starting a new life, connecting with Jesus' story, and joining his people.

The Tightrope Walker

Typically when people first come to faith, they understand only the basics. And that is all that is necessary to begin. Then we start to grow. As Augustine famously said, in a reflection on John 7:17, "Understanding is the reward of faith. Therefore do not seek to understand in order to believe, but believe that you may understand."[25] Faith in God begins with a willingness to believe. Growth in Christian faith involves growth in its understanding dimension, as with the other dimensions as well. As we realize how far we have to go, we should plead, like the father whose son was ill, "I do believe; help me overcome my unbelief!" (Mark 9:24). Just as Jesus responded to the father by addressing his need, so Jesus invites us to receive and to learn from him.

I conclude with some high wire drama. Recently the film *The Walk* has depicted the amazing feat of Philippe Petit who, in 1974, walked 138 feet back and forth eight times on a cable stretched between the tops of the Twin Towers of the World Trade Center in New York.[26] However, a hundred years earlier, another Frenchman, Charles Blondin, crossed the Niagara Gorge on a tightrope some 1,100 feet in length. By one accounting, Blondin made twenty-one crossings on that rope stretched from Prospect Park in the United States to the Canadian side of Niagara Falls. On August 17, 1859, he actually carried his manager across the gorge on his back. As the story goes, one day after he had made such a crossing, he asked the crowd, "Who believes that I can push a man in a wheelbarrow across this gorge?" Everyone cheered enthusiastically. "Now," he asked, "who will get into the wheelbarrow?"

Faith in Jesus has some similarities to Blondin's challenge. Will you get into the wheelbarrow? Perhaps even more, will you allow Jesus to teach you how to walk such a tightrope?

Questions for Reflection and Discussion
1. In an uncertain world, what does it mean for you to risk everything by putting faith in someone or something?
2. List three things you put faith in today or recently. Which one of these required the greatest risk? Why?
3. Describe briefly a situation in which you trusted someone or something and were disappointed. Would you exercise faith like that again? Why or why not?
4. What do you consider your personal "ultimate concern," that is, the core of the worldview you have decided is true? How does this belief affect the way you live?
5. Do you find the argument of this chapter convincing, that faith involves intellect, trust, and action? Why or why not?
6. Which of the three faith elements is strongest for you? Does this make you more liable to one of the distortions?
7. Do any of the faith distortions hit home for you personally? If so, which and why?
8. What would it mean, in terms of faith in Jesus, for you to accept the invitation to walk a tightrope?

Suggestions for Further Reading
Matthew W. Bates, *Salvation by Allegiance Alone: Rethinking Faith, Works, and the Gospel of Jesus the King.* Grand Rapids, MI: Baker Academic, 2017.

Dietrich Bonhoeffer, *The Cost of Discipleship.* 2d ed. New York: Macmillan, 1959.

Thomas H. Groome, "For Christian Faith," ch. 4 in *Christian Religious Education: Sharing Our Story and Vision.* San Francisco, CA: Harper & Row, 1980.

Daniel L. Migliore, *Faith Seeking Understanding: An Introduction to Christian Theology,* 3rd ed. Grand Rapids, MI: Eerdmans, 2014.

CHAPTER 5

God's Design

In the previous chapter, we took a close look at what it means to have *faith* in something or someone. We saw that we do this all the time, that it is virtually impossible to go through a day without putting ourselves at risk to another person, a piece of equipment, and so on. We also saw that faith has three essential components: intellect, trust, and action.

If the story of Blondin, the tightrope walker, is to serve as a parable to challenge our faith in Jesus Christ or whatever worldview you now hold, you will need to consider the content of that worldview. Every worldview functions with a set of core convictions, no matter how random or unrelated these may seem to be at times. It is often a challenge to find a structure to organize such convictions.

In chapter 2, we considered how the Christian narrative, presented in the Bible, answers questions such as Who are we? What's gone wrong? and What time is it? We also noted briefly how Christians and others made statements concerning their beliefs, such as in answer to the question, "What is the prime reality?" The Bible presents its worldview through the *community* (the people of Israel, the followers of Jesus) that formed out of God's interaction and communication with specific human beings. The Bible reflects the dynamic life of that community: its worship, its laws, and its wisdom, as well as its prophetic and apocalyptic writings. These elements are held together through the *story* of God's people, from the accounts of creation (in Genesis and elsewhere in the Bible), human sin and loss of paradise, through the call of Abraham, the adventures of the people Israel, the prophetic anticipation of Messiah, the coming of Jesus as Messiah, and the launch of the church. Together these elements reveal a divine *vision* for the future, embodied in the prophets and in other anticipations. Thus, the Bible guides present decisions of the ongoing community through the community's past and anticipations of its future.

Some Christian worldview basics are listed here, not as a creed (although many of these are found in the creeds of Christian churches), but to present or refer to those things upon which we can rely as we ask questions about what God expects of us and where God might be leading us.

- God made human beings and loves them (Gen. 1–3; John 3:16).
- God is in charge (Isa. 43:10-13; Matt. 5:45).
- God has a claim on our lives (Lev. 20:26).
- God created human beings to love, fear, glorify, and enjoy God and to love one another (Deut. 6:4-5; Pss. 16:11; 34:8; Eccl. 12:13; Matt. 22:36-39; Rom. 15:6-9).
- Human beings are made in God's image and appointed as responsible for creation (Gen. 1:26-29; 2:15). This is part of a pervasive pattern through the Bible in which God seeks to work through people to accomplish divine goals.
- Humanity has failed, and each of us has failed (Eccl. 7:20; Rom. 3:23).
- All human beings need God's forgiveness and restoration (Jer. 33:8; 1 John 1:9); these have been made possible as a gift through the sacrificial death of Jesus on our behalf (Rom. 3:25; 6:23).
- We can have confidence in God's love for us and involvement with us through the life and teachings of Jesus (Matt. 6:25-34; Luke 12:32; John 3:16).
- In the midst of a world that is broken, a world in which death and injustice are indicators of its pain, we can have

hope because Jesus traveled through death to life (Gen. 3:16-19; Eccl. 1:2; 12:8; Rom. 8:10-25; Heb. 2:9, 14).

- God communicates to all people through creation (Ps. 19:1-4; Rom. 1:18-22); all are accountable for living out the life to which God has called us (Matt. 25; Heb. 9:27).
- Each person is called to repent of their sin and seek restoration from God by becoming a follower of Jesus (Matt. 3:2; 16:24; Acts 2:38).
- Jesus is our model of how to live (1 Pet. 2:21; Mark 6:31).
- God is at work in the world, and invites us to be part of that work (Gen. 6:5-14; 18:16-21; 19:13; Judg. 6:11-16; John 5:17-20; Acts 9:1-16).
- God's plan is to work through the church, the body of Christ, on earth; the church is guided by the Holy Spirit (John 16:7-15; Rom. 12:3-8).
- Human beings are given the ministry of reconciling people with God and with one another as they make disciples of Jesus (Matt. 28:18-20; 2 Cor. 5:18; 2 Pet. 3:9).
- The work of human beings participates in the world's brokenness, yet has potential for good (Eccl. 4:9-12).

Four Themes: SCAR

One of the most helpful ways of setting forth the Christian core set of values is called "God's Design" proposed by Elmer A. Martens; it summarizes in four themes many details of God's interaction with the people Israel, Messiah Jesus, and on through the church. These four themes inform us about God's plan, and thus what God is about in the world. Also very importantly, these themes illustrate the program or kingdom in which God invites humans to participate.[27]

From the beginning, God announced that it was not good for human beings to be alone (Gen. 1:27–28; 2:18). From that simple declaration comes the story of God and the people of God that we find in the Bible. A most concise summary of the Bible's plot line might go something like this: God created the universe with a plan involving human beings as key players; humans violated that plan; God put a rescue operation into motion that worked through the community of Israel, hinges on Jesus Christ, and expands through God's community, the church, in anticipation of its final culmination in a new heaven and a new earth.

At a key juncture in this plot line, when Moses was frustrated that God was not being faithful, God announced the four elements that make up God's Design:

> Moses returned to the LORD and said, "Why, Lord, why have you brought trouble on this people? Is this why you sent me? [23] Ever since I went to Pharaoh to speak in your name, he has brought trouble on this people, and you have not rescued your people at all."
>
> [1] Then the LORD said to Moses, "Now you will see what I will do to Pharaoh: Because of my mighty hand he will let them go; because of my mighty hand he will drive them out of his country." [2] God also said to Moses, "I am the LORD. [3] I appeared to Abraham, to Isaac and to Jacob as God Almighty, but by my name the LORD I did not make myself fully known to them. [4] I also established my covenant with them to give them the land of Canaan, where they resided as foreigners. [5] Moreover, I have heard the groaning of the Israelites, whom the Egyptians are enslaving, and I have remembered my covenant. [6] "Therefore, say to the Israelites: 'I am the LORD, and I will bring you out from under the yoke of the Egyptians. I will free you from being slaves to them, and I will redeem you with an outstretched arm and with mighty acts of judgment. [7] I will take you as my own people, and I will be your God. Then you will know that I am the LORD your God, who brought you out from under the yoke of the Egyptians. [8] And I will bring you to the land I swore with uplifted hand to give to Abraham, to Isaac and to Jacob. I will give it to you as a possession. I am the LORD.'" (Exod. 5:22–6:8)

The four themes are community, abundant life, relationship with God, and salvation.

Community. "I will take you as my own people" (v. 7). This is a new expression of what we noted just previously, that it is not good for human beings to be alone. The first man and woman serve as prototype, and almost at once we see the possible breakdowns and complications that follow. God's plan for humans to be together will need to address violations of caring, sharing, and good relations. It will culminate in covenant, first on Mt. Sinai and later on Mt. Calvary (Luke 22:20). God's community requires commitment and account-ability. It necessitates instruction concerning justice, mercy, and worship (Mic. 6:8). It is an opportunity for people to give and receive from one another. It is offered by God, but requires people to take up the challenge to help each other accomplish an ongoing and binding love.

Abundant Life. "I will bring you to the land . . . I will give it to you as a possession" (v. 8). Just as God placed the first two people in the garden, God has a place for Abraham's people that will provide for their essential needs. Israel's connection to land had three important aspects: it was a promise, it was a gift, and it demanded accountability for living justly. It was aimed toward Israel's people but also for those from elsewhere. The land was a tremendous channel of God's abundant and practical blessings to the people, celebrated in festivals and other rituals. It meant caring for restorative justice (Deut. 10). In this area as well as others, Jesus' presentation of God's king-dom had both continuity and discontinuity with what came before him. Significantly, Jesus announced that his kingdom was for all nations, and urged his followers to go (out of the land of Israel and) into all the world to make disciples (Matt. 28:19-20). Unlike some other rabbis, Jesus announces blessings on those outside the land, even outside the people of Israel (Luke 4:25-27). Those who inherit the land will be the meek (Matt. 5:5; Ps. 37:9). In John's Gospel, Israel's institutions, ritu-als, and temple are replaced by Jesus the Messiah (John 2–10). The promise of abundant life, given to Israel initially in connection to land, is still in effect, but it manifests without location on a specific plot of ground (Luke 6:38; Phil. 4:19).

Relationship with God. "I will be your God . . . Then you will know that I am the LORD your God" (v. 7). People need not only each other but also the God who created them. God wishes to enter into a committed relationship with people, both individually and in groups. This relationship is characterized by *knowing*, a term in Hebrew that suggests experiential and emotional awareness and not only information. To know God is to know what God values, including justice for the poor and needy (Jer. 22:13–17).

Salvation. "I will bring you out . . . I will free you . . . I will redeem you" (v. 6). This, the first and most urgent of the four themes for Moses and the Israelite people staggering under bondage in Egypt, was not hinted during the creation. Rather, the other three themes summarize the joyful vision of people in relationship with God, each other, and the abundant creation with which they were to live symbiotically.[28] That is why the acronym SCAR, used to summarize these four themes, can serve as a reminder that God's salvation is a response to a vision damaged, a plan disrupted, a situation in which God must suffer on behalf of a sinful humanity to bring wholeness back again. This renewal, begun symbolically by the clothing of the first man and woman by God as they left the garden (Gen. 3:21), finds its harbinger in Jesus Christ, and its fulfillment at the end of time.

The human choice to separate from God led to brokenness in several ways: between people and people, between people and the creation, and between people and their God. The book of Ecclesiastes is a catalog of the confusing and frustrating paradoxes of life under the sun. Things aren't working right.[29] Humans have a strong sense of justice, yet all fail to live it out themselves. We need and love other people, and yet have a hard time sustaining good relationships, while ultimately we are separated from those we love by death. We have a deep longing for connection with our Creator, yet are also deeply fearful of God as well as confused about just who God is and what God wants of us.

In the midst of this situation, God out of love has a strategy for restoring humans and the rest of creation, a process called *salvation*, which has past, present, and future dimensions. Because God wants people to participate in this effort to heal the brokenness, God called and sent people to be agents of salvation, such as Abraham, Ruth, Moses, David, Huldah, and Isaiah. Ultimately and uniquely, God sent Jesus to live, teach, die, and rise again among us, and to send forth witnesses of restoration and transformation. The good news is that the brokenness of the other three themes may now be restored: human relationships, abundant life, and relationship with God.

God's Design and Two Assignments

Although Exodus 5:22–6:8 is the first articulation of these four elements together in the Bible, a look at the first chapters of Genesis makes clear that community, abundant life, and relationship with God were part of God's original plan for human beings. With human disobedience, salvation became necessary. All four of these continue on through the chapters of Genesis, then come together in this Exodus text. And they may be traced through the rest of the Old Testament and on into the life of Jesus and the church in the New Testament.

God's creation of human beings came with the first of two important assignments, often called the *Creation Mandate* and concerned with providing abundant life. It is presented in two dimensions: to *rule over* creation (Gen. 1:26-28) and to *serve and protect* creation (Gen. 2:15). The fourth theme of God's Design, salvation, aligns with the second major assignment given to human beings, called the *Great Commission* (Matt. 28:18-20). It is the charge Jesus gave to his followers to go make disciples of all the nations.

Thus the two central assignments from God find their context in the midst of God's Design in the world. The Creation Mandate and the Great Commission will be discussed further in chapters 12 and 13, and connected with the two great commandments to love God and neighbor.

Our next chapter takes a closer look at community as something essential to our vocation.

Questions for Reflection and Discussion

1. How do you understand the heart of a Christian worldview?
2. How helpful are the four themes of "God's Design" for summarizing the important information found in the Bible? If there is something missing, what would you add?
3. Which of the four SCAR elements is most interesting or important to you? Why do you think this is the case?

4. State the Creation Mandate and Great Commission in your own words.
5. What do you think about the pattern in the Bible that apparently God wishes to accomplish the divine goals through *people* as much as possible?

Suggestions for Further Reading

Ted Grimsrud, *God's Healing Strategy: An Introduction to the Bible's Main Themes*, rev. ed. Telford, PA: Cascadia, 2011.

Elmer A. Martens, *God's Design: A Focus on Old Testament Theology*, 4th ed. Eugene, OR: Wipf & Stock, 2015.

Scot McKnight, *One.Life: Jesus Calls, We Follow*. Grand Rapids, MI: Zondervan, 2010.

CHAPTER 6

Called in Community

Human beings are social creatures by nature. We find our identity most profoundly in groups, whether in street gangs, the local Rotary Club, or a church fellowship. A person's sense of direction merges with others in ways that are sometimes quite astounding. From a Christian perspective, as Os Guinness has said, "the call of Jesus is personal but not purely individual; Jesus summons his followers not only to an individual calling but also to a corporate calling."[30] In this chapter we take a closer look at the "C" element of the SCAR (God's Design) themes discussed in the previous chapter.

One of the most powerful ways we can help one another understand the truths of life in this world is through stories. Daniel Taylor explains, as noted previously, that stories are prime transmitters of culture, worldview, values, and personal identity. They answer questions such as, Who am I? Where did I come from? Why am I here? Who are you? What will happen to us when we die?[31] This helps us understand why stories are such an important part of the Bible itself. They provide a historical and ideological context for all that God was teaching the people of God—both as individuals and as a whole group—in a variety of situations and a variety of contexts.

Story-Formed Community

A book that can help us understand the way stories shape a group of people is the somewhat odd account of some very savvy rabbits called *Watership Down* by Richard Adams.[32] It details the adventures of a rabbit community as they are uprooted from their warren and seek to form a new residence where it is safe to live. The novel has typical traits found in any adventure story, but what is especially intriguing is the role that stories play in the lives of these very human-like bunnies. Fiver, a small runt of a rabbit, receives some troubling visions that their warren is in imminent danger. Prophet-like, he announces his concerns (which later prove to be true), but they are rejected by the warren's leadership. A small group of rabbits believe him, however, and they travel through a variety of perils until arriving safely at their new home. A number of additional ordeals happen after establishing the new warren, all of which require courage and ingenuity from the otherwise inexperienced rabbits.

It is at these times of serious need and threat that the bunnies draw upon stories they learned in their youth. The best of these stories involve El-ahrairah, a trickster hero, a kind of cross between biblical Jacob and Bugs Bunny. The stories recount situations in which this rabbit, though the odds are always against him, is able to use cleverness to escape and overcome those who are stronger. Telling these stories lifts the rabbits' spirits at difficult times and motivates them to think creatively concerning the particular crisis of the moment.

Another example of the power of story to affect lives is that of *Amistad*. The 1997 film, directed by Steven Spielberg, is based on the true story of the slave ship *La Amistad* and the historical account published by Howard Jones.[33] In 1839, a group of Africans captured in Sierra Leone were sold into slavery in Cuba and chained in the cargo hold of a ship. As the ship crossed the ocean from Cuba to the U.S., Cinqué (Djimon Hounsou), one of the slaves, led a mutiny and took over the ship. The slaves wished to return to Africa but were deceived and intercepted by the U.S. Navy. The forty-four Africans were then imprisoned as runaway slaves and accused of murder for killing most of their captors. A U.S. lawyer took their case and argued successfully that they had been captured and sold illegally, and thus were free citizens. When the case was appealed to the U.S. Supreme Court, former president John Quincy Adams urged for and won their release.

As they wait in prison prior to their trial, the film presents an interesting encounter between some Christians and the slaves. The Christians offer a Bible to the Africans, and, though they cannot read the language, the Africans are intrigued by the pictures found there. In particular, they sense that Jesus sympathizes with the plight of oppressed peoples and is committed to their liberation. Cinqué takes heart as a result and urges that he and his fellow captives be set free. In his circumstances, he embraces the story of Jesus as connected to his own story of suffering with the hope for deliverance.

Both *Watership Down* and *Amistad* show us the importance of stories for giving people a sense of united commitment and purpose. Though Adams has insisted that he did not intend his book as a parable, religious or otherwise, Thomas B. Leininger made the following applications to Christian faith:

- Like the rabbits in *Watership Down*, Christian communities are "story-formed communities" because Christians are people who have been and are being formed by the stories of the Scriptures that culminate in the story of Jesus.
- The converse is also true: the Scriptures are "community formed texts." The Scriptures were formed out of communal experiences of God that were "handed over" (Latin *traditio*) from one generation to another.[34]

Christians need these stories in order to appreciate the significance of God's calling as part of a historic community of faith. Yet, not all Christians think a faith community is necessary.

Community Is Essential
The Reformation launched by Martin Luther when he stood and pounded his ninety-five theses on the church door in sixteenth-century Wittenberg, Germany, resulted in many healthy changes for the ways Christians understand their faith. One of the unfortunate by-products of that change, however, has been a tendency to view the church as a gathering of

convenience. It is seen as a place, for example, where it is easier to find those things that a Christian needs, where Christians can pray for and support each other in helpful ways, but ultimately a collection of people with whom it is not essential to gather. The ultimate realities, Protestants often say, are what Jesus accomplished for us on the cross and the ways in which we personally respond to God through worship, prayer, and witness. Gathering together as a church has advantages and is important, especially for new believers. But when American Protestants in the last thirty years have been asked the question, "Is it necessary to belong to a church to be a Christian?" most have answered "No."

The approach we find to God's people in the Bible is decidedly and consistently just the opposite. And that starts right from the beginning. After God declared everything in creation to be good and *very* good in Genesis 1, we find something that God says is not good: for the man to be alone (Gen. 2:18). This is our first clue that human beings have been created to be together: to live, work, plan, and enjoy life in each other's company. We cannot function well consistently any other way.

We also learn in Genesis, however, that sometimes human collaboration is done in alignment against God rather than cooperating with God's plans. Examples include the way the man and woman disobeyed in the garden (3:6) and the construction of the tower of Babel (Gen. 11:1-9). Nevertheless, God's plans for people are communal. God's response to the problems in Genesis 11 are countered in Genesis 12 when God calls Abram/Abraham and Sarai/Sarah to produce a people, later called Israel, who are God's special instrument to be a blessing to the entire world.

In the New Testament, we see the message over and over again that to be a follower of Jesus means to join with others. The Apostle Paul, for example, says that "there are many parts, but one body. The eye cannot say to the hand, 'I don't need you!' And the head cannot say to the feet, 'I don't need you!'" (1 Cor. 12:20-21). According to the New Testament, important things have changed:

1. Believers in Christ have set aside their primary sense of *belonging* in their biological or sociological family, and have joined the *family of God* (Matt. 12:50; Mark 10:29; Luke 14:26; Gal. 6:10; Eph. 2:19).
2. Believers in Christ have set aside their primary *allegiance* to their country and government, and are now citizens of the *kingdom of God*, one that is already here but not yet here in fullness (Mark 1:15; Eph. 2:19; Phil. 3:20; Col. 4:11).
3. Believers in Christ have set aside their primary *identity* in a cultural or ethnic group, and are now part of the *people of God* (Rom. 9:25-26; 2 Cor. 6:16; Titus 2:14; 1 Pet. 2:9; Rev. 18:4; 21:3).

New Testament scholar Robert Banks puts it this way:

> [F]or Paul the gospel bound believers to one another as well as to God. Acceptance by Christ necessitated acceptance of those whom he had already welcomed (Rom. 15:7); reconciliation with God entailed reconciliation with others who exhibited the character of gospel preaching (Phil. 4:2-3); union in the Spirit involved union with one another, for the Spirit was primarily a shared, not individual, experience (2 Cor. 13:14; Phil. 2:1; Eph. 4:3). . . . To embrace the gospel, then, is to enter into community. A person cannot have one without the other.[35]

One way to summarize this point is to say there is no *Christ* without the *Body of Christ*. This does not mean that Jesus is never accessible to an individual by herself or himself; we can note, for example, the thief on the cross to whom Jesus said, "Truly I tell you, today you will be with me in paradise" (Luke 23:43). Nor does it mean that Jesus' salvation and blessings communicated to us are dependent upon some ritual or other action on our part. But it does mean that Jesus and the New Testament writers never conceived any kind of loner discipleship; rather, a new community of God was being formed. This is evident in nearly every prominent New Testament image used to help us understand God's work through Christ in the world. To these images we now turn.

New Testament Images of the Church

Something essential we must first clarify is that the term *church* in the Bible does *not* refer to a building, which is a common use of that term in English. The New Testament word for "church" is *ekklesia,* which indicates an occasional gathering of people or citizens assembled as a legislative body. In the Greek translation of the Old Testament it can mean a gathering of people for both religious and other purposes. When we come to the New Testament, we discover that *ekklesia* is used of the community of God's people over a hundred times. Yet the nature of the church is too complex to be conveyed by just one word. To capture its significance, the New Testament authors give their readers multiple images, or metaphors, to describe the church. Here are six important clusters of images.[36]

The Church as the People of God. The accent here is on God. God creates and calls people (1 Pet. 2:9-10; Rom. 9:25-26). The term *people* means "people group," a new ethnicity involving all races and nations without devaluing the distinctiveness of each: "Jew *and* Gentile." Terms like "saints," "faithful ones," and "righteous ones" are always plural in the New Testament. They describe the nature of the church rather than the individual Christian life. The church is a saintly community, a "holy people" set apart by and for God. The church is also described as "disciples," "the way," "slaves," "friends," and "witnesses." Basically, the concept of the people of God can be summed up in the promise, "I will be their God and they will be my people" (Heb. 8:10-12).

The Church as a Family. Christians are described using family language, such as "children," "brothers," "sisters," and a "household." Note how the church is often viewed as a collective whole. In the New Testament, the whole gives identity to the individual as well as individuals giving identity to the whole (Matt. 23:9-10; Mark 3:35; 10:29-30; 1 Pet. 2:17; 4:17; 5:9; Heb. 3:1-6; John 1:12; Rom. 16:13-14).

The Church as the New Creation. Another set of images uses cosmic and end times terms: the church is part of a new creation (2 Cor. 5:17). Note that this takes us back to the beginning of time. God is starting over. Other images include the "firstfruits" (Rom. 16:5; 1 Cor. 16:15; James 1:18), the "new humanity" (Eph. 2:11-17; Col. 3:10), "God's Sabbath" (Heb. 4:1-11), and "light" (Matt. 5:14-16; John 12:35; 2 Cor. 4:6; 1 Thess. 5:5; 1 Pet. 2:9). The church is the fulfillment of God's promises. It is so great that cosmic images are used to describe it. These images affirm that God is doing a new thing in the church. God is making all things new. The church is to be the fulfillment of what God intended in the original creation.

The Church as the Body of Christ. The body is an important image in Paul's instruction. The church is a living organism composed of many different complementary members, different but united together. Each member is necessary to the others and to the growth of the whole. Christ is the head of this body. The church grows and matures as different members are properly related to Christ and to each other. This kind of imagery highlights both the *unity* of the church in Christ and the *diversity* of gifts within the one body (1 Cor. 12:12-31; Rom. 12:3-8; Col. 1:18, 24; 2:9-10; Eph. 2:14-16; 3:4-6; 4:4-13).

The Church as a Building. As with body imagery, the images of buildings represent interconnectedness and interrelatedness for a mutual purpose (Heb. 3:6; 10:21). Jesus is the cornerstone, and individual believers are "living stones" as part of this structure (1 Pet. 2:5; 1 Cor. 3:12; Eph. 2:20-22). Also, this new arrangement replaces the temple as the place where God dwells (1 Cor. 6:19; 3:16-17; Eph. 2:21).

The Church as a Team with a Mission. Images such as salt (Matt. 5:13; Col. 4:6), light (Matt. 5:14-16; 6:22-23; 10:27; Luke 2:32), a fragrance (2 Cor. 2:15), or an open letter (2 Cor. 3:2) strongly suggest having a collective impact within one's sphere of influence. Images of actions, such as being ambassadors (2 Cor. 5:20), witnesses (Acts 1:8; 10:39; 10:41; 13:31), reconcilers (Col. 1:20), fishers of people (Matt. 4:19), and colaborers with God (1 Cor. 3:9), further clarify God's intention for believers. Descriptions such as the Jerusalem church growing in numbers daily (Acts 2:41), the Antioch church seeing great numbers of people turning to the Lord (Acts 11:21), and the Thessalonian church having their faith in God known everywhere (1 Thess. 1:8), reflect the church's impact. Paul's teaching to the Ephesian church to prepare God's people for active mission with all the gifts of Christ's body (Eph. 4:11-12) gives support to the missional design of the church. Effective mission involves both word and deed. God's people are mandated to live within a covenant relationship where God is our God and we are God's people demonstrating grace, justice, and faith that works.

Reflection on these image groups reveals how pervasively we find a depiction of unity within plurality: the parts (individual believers) are diverse, but together they accomplish a unified set of tasks. Another element that emerges is function or purpose. The church is set loose on a mission, living in the reality that the kingdom is here, that life is available for all, inviting people to join and to participate in warfare against the kingdom of darkness, while not all recognize or submit to Jesus' lordship.

People who take the name of Jesus have engaged the culture around them in a variety of orientations. (We will investigate six different models of this engagement in ch. 11.) These orientations are relevant not only for those embracing a Christian worldview but in most cases could be employed among those who are committed to other worldviews as well.

Is the Church Part of the Good News?

It could be that this emphasis on the importance of the church for Christian believers is not very cheering. Some people have experienced church as cold, exclusive, boring, and even abusive. People sometimes say they respect Jesus but don't want to be around Christians. Certainly churches are not perfect places. How might we navigate the two realities that God says church is essential and yet churches have problems, even major ones?

This is a big topic, but here are a few ideas. First, we can affirm the basic principle that God wants to draw people together and work through people as a group as well as individually. Second, we can invite God to help us share the love for the church that motivated Paul and other early Christian leaders to help make it as good as possible. Third, we can realize that even Christians in the early years were not perfect and had problems; so the difficulties we see are nothing new. Finally, we can ask God where we should plug in and serve. Although that place won't be perfect, we can trust that God will help meet our needs there and wants to use us there as a blessing to others (even though we aren't perfect either).

This chapter concludes with two stories of Christian activism. One of the glories of the church is that God uses weak and ordinary people in sometimes marvelous ways.

Le Chambon

Our first story takes place in a quaint little town in France. We wouldn't know about the small group of Christians who lived there and their noble actions if it was not for the work of Philip Hallie, professor of philosophy at Wesleyan University, Middletown, Connecticut. As he was working on a project analyzing Nazi cruelty in the early 1970s, he alternated between bitter anger and boredom at the repetitive patterns of oppression. Filled with discouragement, he came across the story of a town of three thousand people in the mountains of southern France, the only place in German-occupied Europe where Jews could find a safe haven. Deeply moved, Hallie found himself weeping in what he later called an instinctive "expression of moral praise."[37]

Hallie, a U.S. soldier in World War II, traveled to France in 1976 to investigate and interview those who remembered and took part in what became the rescue, during the war, of more than five thousand Jewish children. In the village were Huguenots, French Protestants who had experienced persecution for hundreds of years following the revocation of the Edict of Nantes in 1685, a document that previously (from 1598) had given protection to Protestants in France. Their pastor, André Trocmé, and his wife, Magda, using secrecy as their only weapon, encouraged the group as they sheltered and provided for Jews who sought refuge until they could flee France to places of greater safety.

This was challenging not only due to the risk of discovery and the personal cost borne by the villagers, but also because vital resources such as food and clothing were rationed during the war. These allowances had to be stretched further for those guests being harbored in their homes. They followed their consciences; and "what this meant for them was nonviolence. . . . refusing to hate or kill any human being."[38]

Hallie was particularly struck by the way the villagers responded to his interviews. They seemed unable to understand why their actions to protect those in need should be considered something extraordinary. One anecdote is telling in this regard. Eventually the actions of André and his parishioners became known, and two police were sent to his home to arrest him. At the time, the pastor was out, so the policemen waited. As the afternoon passed Magda began to make supper. André returned and prepared to be taken away. But before they left, Magda invited the men to eat a meal. André was then arrested and taken to jail. Later she was asked how she could be so hospitable to those who were there to arrest her husband, to take him away, perhaps to his death. Magda replied simply, "What are you talking about? It was dinner-time; they were standing in my way; we were all hungry. The food was ready. What do you mean by such foolish words as 'forgiving' and 'decent'?"[39]

As Os Guinness describes,

> Hallie came to realize the rightness of a summary by one of his readers: "The Holocaust was storm, lightning, thunder, wind, rain, yes. And Le Chambon was the rainbow." Yes, he concluded, "I realized that for me too the little story of Le Chambon is grander and more beautiful than the bloody war that stopped Hitler."[40]

The Christians of Le Chambon are an example of those who practiced faithfulness for an extended period so that they were ready and able to confront a challenging crisis when it arrived. Hallie also found that the response of the world to their heroic actions is also typical of those who serve in small ways that go under the radar. No crowds and parades honored the townspeople. In fact, after the war André had to make trips and personal appeals to raise money for the training school he felt called to sustain in his home community. One symbol of respect and gratitude for the Christians of Le Chambon, however, is a marker placed at Yad Vashem, the Holocaust memorial in Jerusalem. Otherwise, the significance of what they did is carried only by Hallie's book and those influenced by it.

Timisoara

The second story begins in 1944 when the Soviets overran Romania and named Nicolae Ceausescu, one of the few Communists then in the country, to a leadership role. By the 1970s, he had worked his way through the party and was made president of the country, backed by the army. During his reign, he exported most of Romania's food while its citizens waited in long lines to buy bread baked with sawdust. At the same time, the country's leaders ate sumptuously. Ceausescu implemented a "systematization" plan that saw villages razed and their populations moved to urban centers. There they lived in flimsy apartments with the heat set at fifty degrees during the winter, hot water once per week, electricity limited, and forty-watt bulbs the highest allowed. Families were required to have five children, but because they couldn't afford to feed them, parents felt compelled to give up their babies to two hundred state-run orphanages.

Ceausescu formed a network of secret police whose connections stretched to an estimated twenty-five percent of the country. He required church leaders to clear activities with his Department of Religious Affairs and to report the names of all who attended church services. Church publications praised the regime; prayers were offered that government leaders might prosper. A favorite verse quoted was Romans 13:1, "Let everyone be subject to the governing authorities, for there is no authority except that which God has established. The authorities that exist have been established by God." The government sought to play Christian groups off of each other, giving special privileges to the Orthodox majority while Catholics, Baptists, and other Protestant groups formed a tiny minority.

Not all religious leaders cooperated, however. One such leader was a young pastor of the Hungarian Reformed Church named Laszlo Tokes.[41] In 1987, he became pastor at age thirty-five of a congregation in Timisoara. His predecessor had been a well-known government collaborator, and during his leadership, church membership had dwindled to less than fifty persons. After this man died of a heart attack, Tokes took his place and became quickly popular among both the parishioners and students from the local university.

Tokes brought a new vision to the congregation, a dynamic belief that God wanted to connect with people and give their lives hope. Life at the church blossomed, rituals no longer felt empty, persons were trained in the faith, people were baptized. Within two years, church membership had grown to five thousand. Though the government authorities were not concerned about older people, they became very nervous about the participation of college students. In addition, Tokes gave a televised interview during which he criticized Ceausescu's systematization plan, and particularly the way the Hungarian population was treated by the Romanian government. He was actually suspended by his church superior, but he continued preaching, challenging the government, and the church kept growing.

Tokes also implemented plans for cooperation and joint services with Christians of other denominations, threatening the government's walls erected between religious groups. After a 1988 joint celebration between his church and the Catholic church on October 31 (the day Martin Luther had launched the Reformation), the government stepped up its efforts to challenge and repress. Church members were intimidated, and secret police were stationed both inside and outside of the church when services were held—sometimes with machine guns and visible handcuffs dangling.

Tokes had his ration book denied, his power cut off, his phone made unusable, and visitors to his home were searched. His congregation responded by supplying food and firewood and by communicating secretly. A friend of Tokes who refused to cooperate with the secret police was killed. Others were arrested and beaten. Tokes suffered a knife wound in the face when he and his wife were physically attacked in their home by four men in ski masks. Finally, a court ordered Tokes to be evicted from his home and church, and sent to a small remote village. The date set was December 15, 1989.

On Sunday, December 10, Tokes spoke to his congregation, knowing the high price each paid to worship and remain faithful to their God:

> Dear brothers and sisters in Christ, I have been issued a summons of eviction. I will not accept it, so I will be taken from you by force next Friday. . . . They want to do this in secret because they have no right to do it. . . . Please, come next Friday and be witnesses of what will happen. Come, be peaceful, but be witnesses.[42]

On December 15 the police came to take Laszlo and his wife Edith, but they found that the pastor couple was in the church's apartment, and the church entrance was blocked by church members as well as additional citizens who had joined them. These were hundreds of people of diverse nationalities and a whole variety of different Christian groups. The town's Communist mayor told Tokes he could remain as the church's pastor after all—if the crowd dispersed. But the people didn't trust the mayor. As the standoff continued to one o'clock in the morning, someone brought candles, and the area began to light up in their glow. The demonstration continued through the next day, when people started shouting for liberty and freedom. Eventually some began calling for the removal of Ceausescu. A portion of the crowd moved to the city square.

Before dawn on December 17, the police broke through the crowd, splintered the bolted door of the church, and arrested Tokes, beating his face until it became bloody. Then they took Laszlo and Edith away. At that point, those remaining at the church also moved to the city square where they sang hymns and patriotic songs and held candles through yet another night. Armed troops, dogs, and tanks filled the streets. When the people refused to disperse, the authorities ordered the troops to open fire. Hundreds were shot and at least seventy killed. As protests continued over the next days, something amazing happened: the troops refused orders to fire and actually joined the protestors.

Within four days Ceausescu attempted to flee the country, but was captured and brought to trial. Tokes was restored to church leadership and, in celebration, preached from Isaiah 16:4: "The oppressor will come to an end, and destruction will cease; the aggressor will vanish from the land."

Much more could be told about the Romanian revolution. The protests that began peacefully, and caused the needed spark, eventually turned violent. Other Eastern European revolutions in the late 1980s were achieved with much less violence. Rebuilding the government after the fall of the Communist regime has also had tremendous challenges. Yet the courageous efforts of unarmed citizens, motivated by an allegiance to God more than to a corrupt regime, reveal the power of nonviolent action in a very troubled situation.

Inviting and Engaging

We have just considered two very different accounts of God's people acting for justice that took place in Le Chambon and Timisoara. Both demonstrate that inviting people to join the kingdom of God is not simply declaring a message. Rather, it urges them to be part of God's drama until Jesus returns. In the process, such persons become members of a new people and family, and, therefore, a new culture. Each shares in a corporate as well as an individual witness. This witness is organic, ongoing, flowing naturally from a Christian way of life. It engages and even partners with others to bring God's light to the world, while holding onto a different core set of understandings and values.

Questions for Reflection and Discussion
1. Why do people need a community of other people?
2. What community or communities are most significant for you? Why are these important for you?
3. How do stories play a role in reinforcing the importance of that community or group for you?

4. Which community story in this chapter is most interesting to you? Why do you find it interesting?
5. How do you react to the phrase, "There is no Christ without the body of Christ?" Does this accurately reflect what the New Testament teaches? If not, how would you explain the role of community for Christian faith?
6. Regarding the six clusters of New Testament images that describe the church, what insights or understandings seem most important to you?
7. What does it mean to you that Christians no longer find their primary identity in family, nation, or ethnic group? Are these connections still important? How?

Suggestions for Further Reading

Richard Adams, *Watership Down*. London: Rex Collings, 1972.

Robert Banks, *Paul's Idea of Community*, 2nd ed. Peabody, MA: Hendrickson, 1994.

Philip P. Hallie, *Lest Innocent Blood Be Shed*. New York: Harper & Row, 1979.

Stanley Hauerwas, "A Story-Formed Community: Reflections on *Watership Down*," in *A Community of Character*, 9–35. Notre Dame: University of Notre Dame Press, 1981.

Alan Kreider, *The Patient Ferment of the Early Church: The Improbable Rise of Christianity in the Roman Empire*. Grand Rapids, MI: Baker Academic, 2016.

Paul S. Minear, *Images of the Church in the New Testament*. Philadelphia, PA: Westminster, 1960.

Daniel Taylor, *Tell Me a Story: The Life-Shaping Power of Our Stories*. St. Paul, MN: Bog Walk, 2001.

Laszlo Tokes and David Porter, *The Fall of Tyrants*. Wheaton, IL: Crossway, 1990.

Part 2
What Is True, What Is Good

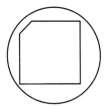

CHAPTER 7

Navigating Postmodernism

In part 2 of this book (chs. 7–11), we consider some of the most challenging questions related to what is true and what is good in order to situate our sense of vocation within these larger issues. The last chapter in this section, chapter 11, provides some history and some options for engaging our culture.

In our previous discussion of worldviews (ch. 2), we noted that they can be described in two major ways: as a set of propositions (statements of what people believe to be true) and as a narrative (a story that portrays what is true). Those who adopt a form of Naturalism, the belief that the material world—matter and energy—is all that exists, typically embrace evolution, not only as an explanation of the diversity of life but also as a story that accounts for the entirety of our existence.[43] The story begins with some inert matter that gets stirred up and energized so that a small life form is produced. This life form reacts to its environment, develops, and reproduces. Randomly, over millions of years, different forms grow, change, and become more complex. But not every form of life survives—only the fittest. That is, life is about competition, about winners and losers, so that this is an exciting and dramatic underdog scenario. Despite all odds, complex life, and ultimately human beings, find their way into the world with all its splendor. It is a simple story, yet can be emotionally compelling; in fact, it *has* been embraced and *has* influenced many aspects of Western understanding.

Another Naturalist tale responds to those who believe in the supernatural, in God or the gods. The story, told originally by John Wisdom, goes like this:

> Two people return to their long neglected garden and find, among the weeds, that a few of the old plants are surprisingly vigorous. One says to the other, "It must be that a gardener has been coming and doing something about these weeds." The other disagrees and an argument ensues. They pitch their tents and set a watch. No gardener is ever seen. The believer wonders if there is an invisible gardener, so they patrol with bloodhounds, but the bloodhounds never give a cry. Yet the believer remains unconvinced, and insists that the gardener is invisible, has no scent, and gives no sound. The skeptic doesn't agree, and asks how a so-called invisible, intangible, elusive gardener differs from an imaginary gardener, or even no gardener at all.[44]

This parable challenges those who believe in God to explain how their conviction differs from belief in something that doesn't actually exist. One approach to such an explanation by one who believes in the gardener would be to point to what actually takes place in the garden: Are things being fertilized? Are things happening that cannot be easily explained if no gardener exists? Parables such as this one can be a great stimulus for significant conversations.

A different story represents our Pluralist era better than the two above: the ancient Indian tale of the blind men and the elephant. Here is one version of the story:

> Six blind men sought out an elephant and wanted to understand what it was like. The first leaned against his side and decided the animal was like a wall. The second felt the tusk and said the elephant was like a spear. The third felt the trunk and declared the beast to be like a snake. The fourth felt one of the legs and was convinced the animal was like a tree. The fifth touched the ear and decided the elephant was like a fan. Finally, the sixth blind man felt the tail and stated that the animal was like a rope.[45]

All six encountered the same animal but only part of it, and so came away with a different description. Because the men did not share their experiences, they were unable to reconstruct the full truth about the elephant.

On one level, this story reminds us of our need for humility and to be open to learning from the experience of others. Pluralists, however, believe that this tale is definitive of the human condition: we will never fully understand or agree on what is real as long as groups isolate themselves and insist they alone have all the truth. What this punch line requires, however, is that someone (the king and his court in the original version) is actually able to see both the elephant and the individual parts encountered by each of the men, something none of the blind men is able to do. The parable as used by Pluralists presumes on the perspective available from a sighted person while insisting that the six men represent all of humanity, none of whom are sighted. Thus, Pluralism is one more example of claiming to see while others are blind.[46]

The Christian faith offers a different story, an account of God who created the world and appointed human beings to be its stewards. These persons disobeyed, causing paradise to be lost and tremendous turmoil to begin. As part of God's plan to repair this brokenness, God called Abraham and Sarah to form a family; God instructed, disciplined, and directed this group over nearly two thousand years, promising that a Messiah (anointed leader) would someday come. Christians testify that Jesus is that person, who lived and taught among the people of first-century Palestine, allowed himself to be arrested and killed, and was raised to life by God's power. Jesus then commissioned his disciples to receive the Holy Spirit and to give witness as they make disciples of all people. Jesus will return, bringing God's kingdom to fulfillment, and initiating the final transformation of our world and its inhabitants.

Whether you come to this chapter having no commitment to Christian faith, a recent commitment, or many years in the Christian family, you may wonder which worldview actually *is* correct. If faith means taking a risk, it is not surprising that we sometimes ask ourselves whether faith in God is really justified. How do we know who or what to trust? Can we be sure God exists? On what basis can nontheistic worldviews be ruled out? Can we be sure that we should risk our entire life to follow a special person, whether Jesus Christ or anyone else?

In this chapter, we will consider ways of addressing questions like these, but first it is important to realize that such doubts are not only normal, they are actually important to face and to think about. In fact, such questions do not necessarily indicate that someone lacks faith. They may indicate that the person is open to faith, or that faith is trying to hang on and grow in maturity. Anyone who wishes to be a follower of Jesus with integrity is bound to face challenges in his or her spiritual walk. And being sure we have placed our "ultimate concern" faith in the right object is one of them.

Postmodernism: What Changed?

As described in chapter 2, a worldview is a set of assumptions that operate like a lens enabling us to interpret the world. A worldview can be discerned by what a person believes (often stated as propositions), by symbols a person adopts, stories that a person finds important, and actions that a person does. These elements are clues to how a person believes the universe is constructed and the values at the heart of those constructions.

Western culture, in the past several centuries, has experienced some dramatic shifts in the way persons approach their world. These shifts have an effect on everyone. A person who embraces a given worldview can have that understanding affected by what is sometimes referred to as "the spirit of the age." John Dewey offered a propositional description of such shifts. The first era we will call *Premodern*. The first shift, what we will call *Modern* (or Naturalism), burst on the scene in the Enlightenment of eighteenth-century Europe.[47] The second shift, *Postmodern*, arose in the twentieth century. Dewey presents four categories in which change was particularly noticeable from the *Premodern* to the *Modern*.[48] In the chart below, the issues are extended also to the *Postmodern* era.

PROPOSITIONAL	Premodern	Modern	Postmodern
God/Supernatural	Yes	No, or Deist	Maybe
Human Authority	Fixed institutions (church, monarchy)	Human mind	Human mind unreliable, but all we have
Time Focus	Past	Future (progress)	Present (no progress likely)
Source of Truth	Traditional wisdom	Scientific method	Listen to many voices

As mentioned above, stories are also a way to recognize differences in worldviews. Robert Jenson notes that Western culture for hundreds of years in the Premodern era was dominated by a common story, the story carried by the Jewish and Christian Bibles.[49] This story said that there was a God who created the world, loved the world, held the world accountable to certain values and standards, and sought to rescue human beings from the problems in which they found themselves.

NARRATIVE	Premodern	Modern	Postmodern
Common Story	Jewish/Christian	Jewish/Christian	None
Storyteller	God	None	Many

The Enlightenment accepted the basic elements of that story but sought to remove the storyteller, that is, rejected the notion that the Creator God was someone to whom humans were accountable. The loss of the storyteller eventually led to loss of the universal story at the center of Western culture. Postmodernity believes in the concept of a storyteller, but not a universal one. Postmodern people tend to be suspicious that the attempt to rally around a universal story and storyteller is a disguised way of controlling others. Therefore, they listen to the variety of stories and can appreciate them as long as none of them tries to be universal. Or we could say that the preferred *story* is one in which people tells stories without any being privileged over the other.

In this version of Pluralism, people become suspicious if anyone attempts to impose their story on others, wondering what that person may have to gain. Jenson urges Christians to embody their story, and to retell it regularly, without imposition, in order to witness to a world that is lost.

We should note that despite these major shifts in Western culture, adherents of all three approaches—Premodern, Modern, and Postmodern—survive among us. However, the predominant orientation right now is the latter, and what it offers us is primarily suspicion. "Look out!" it says, "There's a lot of danger and people who will try to manipulate you." Warnings can be helpful, notably the concern that logic and rhetoric can be used to selfishly control others. But caution in itself offers little positive upon which to base our lives, and we need logic to evaluate the evidence in plain sight before us.

How to Respond

As we consider the worldview turmoil of our time, how should we respond? Does evidence exist that we should consider as we evaluate the claims of competing worldviews? In light of our faith discussion in chapter 4, what would it take, for example, to embrace genuine faith in Jesus? We noted that such faith would have an intellectual dimension, believing that Jesus is the Messiah, the Son of God, the Savior of the world. Such faith would also mean placing trust in Jesus, allowing him to guide one's life, listening to his teachings, learning to be like him. And third, such faith in Jesus would mean actually doing what Jesus teaches, taking up one's cross and following.

The next chapter examines what Jesus had to say on these issues. The remainder of the current chapter reflects on four aspects of universal human experience in search of clues by which to discern among the various worldview options.

Signposts

As we have noted previously, faith in God as the Bible presents it does not mean committing to something without any evidence. When God laments a lack of faith in someone or some group, God often mentions how they turned away *despite* all the evidence given to them (Isa. 5:1-4; Jer. 7:25-26; cf. Matt. 11:20-24). God did not expect them to act in faith without reasons. N. T. Wright, in his book *Simply Christian*, describes four "signposts," four experiences common to humanity: justice, spirituality, relationships, and beauty.[50] Which worldview, we might ask, best accounts for these human experiences? And especially the value we give to each, and the longing we have for all four? We will now examine each in turn.

Justice. Human beings have a strong sense of right and wrong. This is evident from the most ancient law codes to the children playing in your neighborhood. How easily do the words, "That's not fair," emerge in everyday contexts! They are codified in our policies, they appear to be written on our hearts. Yet just as noticeable is the reality that human beings break laws (reflecting one reason why laws are needed), abuse one another (sometimes the abuser is *protected* by law), and inflict genocide in various parts of the globe. The Holocaust of the Jews as well as the Palestinian Nakba, along with the exploitation done to African Americans, Native Americans, and First Nation people should be vivid in our consciousness. Our economic systems allow the number of billionaires in the world to increase even as billions of people struggle to find basic food and clean water.

While it is encouraging that sometimes justice is done— that is, we see criminals apprehended and punished, or regimes such as South Africa's apartheid dismantled—we are further troubled by natural disasters; tsunamis, earthquakes, tornados, and hurricanes also are "not fair." They cripple, take lives, and destroy property worth millions of dollars regardless whether the victims are morally admirable or not. Perhaps most troubling, if we will be honest with ourselves, is that when we look inside, we discover we too are guilty of violating those things we know to be good and right. We need forgiveness or we shall remain broken. We need to be changed, or we shall keep on breaking.

Several major ways are offered to explain this pervasive sense of morality among human beings. One is that morality has simply evolved, developed within the fittest surviving organisms as they grew from simple to complex. Yet it is difficult to account for certain moral motivations on the grounds that it improved survival value, such as the motivation to sacrifice oneself for another who is in danger. A second explanation is that morality is a fantasy, and those who recognize it as such can improve their lifestyle at the expense of those who do not. From this perspective, Machiavelli and Nietzsche proposed that one should grab as much power as surreptitiously as possible. Again, it seems that those who believe in morality would gradually be eliminated.

A third approach is that our commonly discerned morality is a dream from another reality, one that has little impact on our present circumstances but by which one can be consoled that a better experience will one day be ours. The second and third approaches motivate passivity for the oppressed and motivate others to grasp for power, enhancing a cycle of violence. A fourth approach says that the morality we recognize originates from elsewhere, and that source has potential to enable change toward justice and other moral good, both now and in the future.

Christians, Jews, and Muslims take this last option. For Christians, Jesus is the embodiment (also called *incarnation*) of this source. His teaching advocated God's justice, he lived and acted justly, and in his death he absorbed in himself the world's injustices. On this basis—an acknowledgement that all people are guilty before God, yet forgiven by God—human beings have the potential to resolve their acts of injustice toward each other by refusing to inflict any more. Followers of Jesus are called to embody this way of living to show the world a different way of justice, and thus to follow in Jesus' steps (1 Pet. 2:21). It was devout Christians John Woolman and William Wilberforce who championed the abolition of slavery in the U.S. and Britain respectively. Martin Luther King Jr.

championed a Christian vision to continue the fight against bigotry and racism. The decades-long campaign of Christian leaders such as Bishop Desmond Tutu against apartheid in South Africa resulted in power transfer with little bloodshed and the implementation of restorative justice through the Truth and Reconciliation Commission. Other Christian martyrs for causes of justice include Dietrich Bonhoeffer in Nazi Germany and Oscar Romero on behalf of the poor in El Salvador. The Christian worldview both accounts for and provides motivation for this signpost of justice in human experience.

Spirituality. Human beings are incurably religious. We see evidence of this in early human cultural remains, and it persists around the globe today. Two ideologies have tried to ignore and suppress this human characteristic. In the West, Naturalist philosophy has insisted that matter and energy are all that exist. In the East, Marxist political regimes imposed this Naturalism by suppressing religious expression. For about one hundred years, these ideologies attempted to pave over with concrete the bubbling springs of spiritual desire. And then, like a geyser in Yellowstone Park, the springs burst forth.

In the West, this bursting has taken a diversity of forms, some ancient such as Tarot cards, crystals, and horoscopes, as well as various versions of fundamentalism, and some newer formulations, such as the so-called New Age religions and belief in spiritual vortexes. In the East, the bursting revealed that religious belief had merely gone underground and was never eliminated. The burstings forth have been messy and complicated. Militant groups of various backgrounds claim divine inspiration and support for their causes. From websites, to book clubs, to spirituality sections in bookstores, we see evidence that humans hunger for something beyond or behind the natural world.

Of course, this description has not accounted for other parts of the world. In Africa, the Middle East, parts of the Far East, and Central and South America, various forms of religion and spirituality have continued to be practiced. While many of these forms seem primitive and puzzling to Western minds, they are further evidence that spiritual longings are manifest in all cultures.

Christians account for spiritual hunger as a symptom that humans were created for some kind of interaction with their Creator. Therefore, the evident human craving in our time and all times is completely expected. Augustine, in his Confessions, said of God, "You made us for yourself and our hearts find no peace until they rest in you."[51] C. S. Lewis put it this way,

> God designed the human machine to run on Himself. He Himself is the fuel our spirits were designed to burn, or the food our spirits were designed to feed on. There is no other. That is why it is just no good asking God to make us happy in our own way without bothering about religion. God cannot give us a happiness and peace apart from Himself, because it is not there. There is no such thing.[52]

Relationships. People need people, and most of us know it. As N. T. Wright summarizes,

> It seems that we humans were designed to find our purpose and meaning not simply in ourselves and our own inner lives, but in one another and in the shared meanings and purposes of a family, a street, a workplace, a community, a town, a nation. When we describe someone as a "loner," we're not necessarily saying the person is bad, simply that he or she is unusual.[53]

We deeply long for and treasure our relationships with others, and are deeply hurt, even terribly tormented, when they are lost. Such loss can come in a variety of ways, perhaps most harshly through rejection. Lovers proclaim eternal love and commitment, and yet in some cases their marriage, so joyfully begun, ends in divorce. Friendships are another source of great happiness, and family, for many, is the center of their emotional existence. Yet even the most wonderful and committed of relationships often have their difficulties and trials. How can something be so important to us and yet so hard to deal with? Furthermore, all relationships end in death, something

Western people in particular often try futilely to deny. As one caption put it, "Death Rate Holding Steady at 100%." Why are people relationships so significant and yet so fragile?

Christians understand why we value others so much. It is part of the way God designed humans to function. Though our level of interest in being together differs according to culture and personality, it is not good to be alone (Gen. 2:18). Among the monotheistic faiths only Christianity has claimed that the one God involves multiple persons, called the *Trinity*. This concept explains how God can be love, for love requires both giving and receiving. Humans by extension are instructed to love one another, not because we don't want to but because eventually it becomes so difficult. Mostly this is due to the brokenness of humanity not fully connected to its Creator. But the fragility of life is also part of human brokenness. Christians affirm the triumph of Jesus over death through his crucifixion and resurrection. Though death remains an enemy until the end, death will be defeated (1 Cor. 15:26).

The drive we feel toward human relationships, despite their challenges and transience, is another signpost pointing to that which is true.

Beauty. One time I was sitting with a friend watching a magnificent sunset. We commented to each other about the beautiful orange and blue colors, the swirls in the midst of clouds, the amazing display that filled the western sky so rapturously. As the minutes went by, however, I began to notice that the sunset was not quite as striking as it had been previously. And as it declined further, the sky became a pleasant, but quite commonplace, splash of color. What changed? What was lost? How did we recognize something called "beauty" that ascended for a moment and then receded before our eyes?

Humans are fascinated with beauty in a variety of forms, and we see evidence of this in the earliest human remains: bracelets, necklaces, and other jewelry, pictures painted on cave walls, figurines. We celebrate good art, we sponsor beauty contests, and even the graffiti on passing boxcars has its own artistic flair. We become absorbed by music, we enjoy the sound of birds, we love the smell of flowers and food. We attend films and plays, we take care to adorn ourselves with colorful clothing. Yet, oddly, beauty, like humanity itself, is transient. This is partly because human splendor fades with time, despite the desperate (and sometimes grotesque) attempts of aging people to hold onto it. But even more perplexing, as much as humans delight in beauty, they cannot always agree on what *is* beautiful. Considerations of beauty in one culture are not always appreciated in another, whether separated by geography or time. The glamour models of one era may be little regarded in the next. Yet for most of us, experiences of beauty, whether visual or otherwise, are very important. And they are precious; they come in pockets or brief glimpses. Even their memory can be a source of great joy.

Wright likens our situation to the hypothetical discovery of a lost piece of music by Mozart. The work turns out to be the piano portion of a composition involving another instrument or instruments, perhaps an oboe or cello. The piano element is beautiful, yet it points to something even more wonderful: the combined piece of music as originally composed. And thus it is frustratingly incomplete. Likewise, the world is full of beauty, but the beauty is incomplete, only another echo of a voice whose message is unclear.

The Christian faith accounts for the significance of beauty as a signpost, a manifestation of the beauty of God shown in all that God has created. The Bible's Creator is a great artist, filling the world with color, joy, pleasure, diversity, and exhilaration, from amazing microscopic items to the glory of the planets, galaxies, and nebulae. For C. S. Lewis, such experiences were part of following the clues that led him to the God of the Bible. He used the German word *Sehnsucht*, a deep desire, to describe such experiences.[54] It is like hearing the echo of a voice, or longing for a country one has never seen. The desire brings pain, but a pain we want to have because the longing itself is pleasurable. It is God's way of hindering people from becoming satisfied with the world as it is now because our real home will require God's transforming work (Heb. 11:13-16; Rev. 21).

But the significance of beauty is not obvious, and it can be accounted for in other ways. Maybe it is just some emotional trigger inside that has no larger connection. But I will challenge you as my pastor once challenged me. Read the words of the Bible texts that Handel incorporated into his masterwork, *Messiah*. Then go to a live performance. Does the music add something, in fact, something powerful? A worldview that cannot account for the significance of beauty is truly impoverished.

Signposts and Paradoxes

To sum up these four (possible) signposts, paradoxes are found in each. Humans insist on justice, yet we must admit that each of us fails at some point. We are incurably spiritual so that no concrete can hold such a geyser, yet our religious impulses burst forth as much in violence as in celebration of an awesome world. We desperately need relationships with others, yet allowing them to flourish is often terribly difficult. Further, this most important of treasures ends in death, the seemingly final separation. Beauty in its various forms is also wonderful yet transient, and there is no consensus either on what is beautiful or the significance of beauty.

Despite the complications, these four experiences are universal enough to human existence that they demand some kind of accounting. Is there a worldview that takes our attitudes toward them into account in a satisfying way? It is worthwhile to evaluate your worldview in regard to them.

We turn now to consider what Jesus taught and modeled concerning what is true and where to place our faith.

Questions for Reflection and Discussion

1. What do you believe is "really real"? Why?
2. What things do you believe in that cannot be seen? Why do you believe in them anyway?
3. Do you believe in God? Why? How would you try to convince someone that God exists? How would you describe God?

4. How do you respond to the invisible gardener parable? Is there "gardening" going on in the world? What is happening that is best explained by positing a Gardener?
5. Are the four "signposts" worth considering when evaluating your personal worldview? Which of the four are most significant for you?
6. What explanations are there for the signposts other than the Christian answers? Which answers are most persuasive for you?

Suggestions for Further Reading

Robert W. Jenson, "How the World Lost Its Story." *First Things* 36 (October 1993): 19–24.

C. S. Lewis, *The Pilgrim's Regress*, 3rd ed. Grand Rapids, MI: Eerdmans, 1943.

N. T. Wright, *Simply Christian: Why Christianity Makes Sense.* San Francisco, CA: HarperCollins, 2006.

CHAPTER 8

Getting a Handle

In the previous chapter, we noted the loss of confidence that has led to Postmodernism and how it offers few answers to big questions. We also reviewed four possible "signposts" in human experience that we do well to ponder. We consider now how Jesus helps us know where a risk is worth taking for our faith. This includes honestly looking at ourselves, facing up to frustrating experiences in our lives, considering the importance of testimony as evidence, and examining the issue of Jesus' identity. The chapter concludes with a few additional reflections on coming to thoughtful faith decisions.

Soil Analysis

Jesus gives us a clue why people can fail to reach faith in the truth though they have adequate evidence. In one of his parables, he told about the seed of God's Word being scattered. When it landed on good soil, it took root and produced a good harvest but not in other cases. Some soil had weeds, some had rocks, and in some cases the soil was hard and the birds snatched away the seed (Mark 4:1-20). This suggests that something about a person's receptivity makes a difference.

Returning to considerations related to the justice signpost, we might ask whether there is a *moral* factor to faith. A person must be *willing* to believe the good news. Jesus said, "Anyone who chooses to do the will of God will find out whether my teaching comes from God or whether I speak on my own"

(John 7:17). What Christian faith requires is demanding and may cause us to hesitate. As G. K. Chesterton wrote, "The Christian ideal has not been tried and found wanting. It has been found difficult and left untried."[55]

We need to ask ourselves, as honestly as possible, whether there are things we want very much *not* to know are true. This could be because we would then need to make changes in our life. While some of those changes might be welcome, others might not. It seems easier to stay ignorant. It is somewhat like the approach some persons take to physical health. There may be something wrong with their body, but if they go to the clinic, the doctor might advise a change in diet or some unpleasant therapy. So, they reason, if they don't make an appointment, they won't have to change. Of course, one could point out to such a person that ignorance might result in something much worse than therapy or a change in diet. It could lead to terrible suffering and/or premature death.

Similarly in the case of our soil. Do we really not want to know the truth about who we are? Better to find out now. Better to cultivate the soil, pull out the weeds, or otherwise prepare for that good seed that alone can give us life. Truth has a moral element (John 7:17). We are accountable for our willingness to know the truth.

Suffering, Wrestling, and Lamenting

Another complication in the faith arena is that bad situations may arise that do not make sense. They then may become roadblocks when considering a worldview such as Christianity, which claims that a powerful benevolent God oversees our universe. Sometimes we encounter tremendous suffering: physical, emotional, or both. We may find ourselves with a mixture of responses in such cases, including tremendous anger. We might not even know where our anger is targeted, although sometimes the target is clear: those who have abused or otherwise harmed us. But at whom should we be angry for a natural disaster, or the unexplained death of a loved one, or the divorce of one's parents? In such cases the world can seem cruel, mystifying, crazy, and utterly cold.

There is no way to adequately address such very terrible and important experiences in this small space. What I offer here is a summary of what has been helpful to me in the midst of my searching. I found it unexpected yet reassuring that the Bible records the experiences of numerous individuals who likewise found life and their relationship with God to be puzzling and frustrating. I was also impressed by what they did in response: mainly two things that I will call *wrestling* and *lamenting*.

The wrestling image comes from Genesis 32 where Jacob physically wrestled with an unknown assailant, and insisted that this man (or angel or God) bless him. He survives the encounter, blessed but with a limp. I believe we are similarly invited to struggle through with God in difficult times. Like Jacob, we should refuse to let go until we have something to show for it. This experience takes different forms, but for many the story of Jacob has served as an analogy to their own life.

Lamenting is found throughout the Bible. What we typically discover in such cases is that the person, trying to be faithful but confused, cries out in anger or frustration to God (e.g., Hab. 1:2-4). In fact, half of the prayers in the Bible's book of Psalms lament that things are not going as they should. We also find lament from the saints in the book of Revelation (Rev. 6:10).

I found it encouraging to notice God's response to persons in such situations. God does not judge or criticize them (e.g., Num. 11:10-17; Job 42:7-8; Jer. 12). The difficulty of their situation is acknowledged. They are affirmed in their frustration and confusion. But notice what comes next: they are then challenged to continue their lives on the basis of their *previous* experience of God's dependability. And in many cases, they are given a new assignment, in effect a further test of their faith, though the assignment itself might be very small.

What is evident throughout the Bible is also present in Jesus' life and teachings in these two areas. Jesus had his own wrestling in Gethsemane, he followed through with his assignment that led to the cross, and he lamented on the cross, quoting from Psalm 22. In short, the Bible never presents a picture of life embracing God and God's direction that is free from pain and uncertainty. The challenge is to have faith in the midst of such a life, and the promise is that we will come through on the other side.

The Significance of Testimony

Have you ever stopped to consider how much of what you know is based on information you have received from someone else? Are you pretty sure the world is a round ball rather than flat like a table? On what basis have you come to that conclusion? Vitamins, vegetables, and oatmeal are good for you, or so you've been told. If you are convinced that a certain make of automobile is superior to others, you may have been told that by people whose judgment you trust, or you may have read test results from reliable testing agencies.

The Bible is also full of testimony (e.g., John 20:30-31; 21:24). The person who is confronted with this evidence must then decide whether the testimony and the ones giving it have integrity. If a person is selling something, we want to know what is in it for them. Is it a commission or some other monetary reward? Testimony with high credibility comes from those who have nothing obvious to gain personally from what they hope you will believe or do. We give even higher credibility to those who have embraced something knowing it will be to their disadvantage.

Likewise we can examine Jesus himself. He encouraged those around to evaluate the evidence through testimony that pointed to him (John 5:31-47; 10:25; 15:26-27). So, does what we hear about him suggest someone who can be trusted? Does his love for children, fearlessness before those in power, ministry of healing, teaching, caring relationships, and willingness to suffer death rather than harm others encourage us to pay attention to him? Similarly for those who claim that Jesus is God's Messiah and that he died and came back to life again three days later. Did they have something to gain? Actually, they had a lot to lose, and it appears they suffered and lost their lives as they told others about this Jesus. Today also many who take Jesus' name suffer as a result. By most standards, testimony about Jesus has high credibility.

Additional Aspects of Jesus and Truth

We now consider some additional faith matters that are connected with statements of Jesus.[56] Jesus announced, "I am the truth" and claimed that the reason he "came into the world [was] to testify to the truth" (John 14:6; 18:37). To align with truth requires knowing him. Jesus challenged people to evaluate carefully before choosing to be his disciple (Luke 14:25-33). This involves using our minds and acknowledging certain facts as true. Yet a relationship with a person also goes beyond a creed or a list of statements. It involves engagement; it is something that grows, changes, and develops. This relationship with Jesus will motivate us to know as much as we can about what he said and what he did.

Jesus promised the Holy Spirit who would come and "guide you [plural] into all the truth" (John 16:13). That means we will need one another and can expect to learn from others. The body of Christ has members with gifts of wisdom and knowledge (1 Cor. 12:8) as well as teaching (Rom. 12:7). But all share in this growth process (1 Cor. 14:26; Col. 3:16). Truth can never be solely individual, either as a list of objective facts or as some internal subjective determination, though both are important.

Jesus said two things that specifically point to the relationship between obedience and truth. He told Pilate, "Everyone who belongs to the truth listens to my voice" (John 18:37). To "listen" in this way means to respond by acting on it. This is the action element of faith. What we believe we live out. Related to this, Jesus said, "If you continue in my word, you are truly my disciples; and you will know the truth, and the truth will make you free" (John 8:31-32). Truth is liberating: it brings wholeness and breaks bondages.

Jesus and Questions

Our discussion concerning Jesus has so far considered what Jesus had to say. For the Christian worldview, Jesus is the center. Christians need to know what Jesus did and what Jesus said, and when it comes to anything else, even anything else in the Bible, it matters a lot what Jesus thought about it, if we have any clues to that at all.

It is not surprising, then, that when we study the Gospels, where we find more about Jesus than anywhere else (in the Bible or out of the Bible), we discover that Jesus is the question, *the* question. So let's take a look at the issue of Jesus' identity.

Martin Copenhaver, in his book, *Jesus Is the Question*, cites some interesting statistics:

> In the Gospels Jesus asks 307 questions. By contrast, he is asked only 183 questions. Most striking of all, Jesus gives direct answers to only eight of those 183 questions he is asked.[57]

The first utterances we hear from Jesus are questions (Luke 2:46-49), asking teachers in the temple and asking his anxious parents (who were searching for him) why they didn't expect him to be there. At the end of his life, he asks a question of God while hanging on the cross: Why have you forsaken me? (Mark 15:34). Jesus rises from the dead on Easter and begins asking more questions (e.g., Luke 24:17, 19, 26, 38, 41; John 20:15, 29; 21:5, 15, 16, 17, 22).

What should we make of this information? Statistics in themselves can be misleading. Some of Jesus' questions are what we would call *rhetorical*: they intend to make a point rather than to invite a response. Certainly Jesus had plenty to teach. His Sermon on the Mount is packed with important information. His parables bear continued study and reflection.

But notice his style. He engages people in conversation. He invites them to *think* about important issues. In many situations, he seems more eager to ask questions than to give information. Both his parables and his questions are ways of motivating people to dig deep within themselves—to determine whether they care enough to learn about themselves, about life, and about the God who created them. His indirect answers accomplish a similar function, as when he responds to a man's question, "Who is my neighbor?" by telling a story about a traveler who encountered a wounded man on the road to Jericho. "So," Jesus in conclusion asked the man whose question elicited the story, "*who was a neighbor* to the wounded man?" When Jesus changed the question, the man could recognize that a Samaritan, whom he no doubt found disgusting, was his new role model (Luke 10:25-37).

Three of the questions Jesus answers directly concern law in the Bible (e.g., you must forgive 490 times not just seven). Another has to do with the greatest commandment: love God! When asked by Peter who will betray him, he indicates Judas.

Jesus Is the Question

These descriptions and accounts of Jesus are packaged into four books we call the Gospels whose major point is to invite us to answer Jesus' *most important* question, "Who do you say I am?" (Matt. 16:15; Mark 8:29; Luke 9:20; cf. John 18:37; 20:31). This, in fact, is the last question to which Jesus gives a direct answer. The high priest asked, "Are you the Messiah, the Son of the Blessed One?" Jesus answered, "I am" (Mark 14:61-62). For, as Copenhaver correctly recognizes, Jesus is *the* question. Each of us must make a decision about his identity.

What are the options? Most people in our world are content to consider Jesus a good moral teacher. Fortunately for the world, we have such teachers, even great ones that we call prophets. And such people help us to realize that we have gone in a bad direction, that we should turn around and be better people. So that is one option: a moral teacher, perhaps a great one. A second option, as C. S. Lewis famously challenged us to consider, is that he is a crazy man, someone claiming to be important, even divine, who is deluded and needs medication or to be institutionalized. The world has plenty of those, and we don't need one more. Third, he might be a charlatan, a fraud. We also have plenty of those. People who deceive in order to get our money or abuse us in some other way. With the first option, Jesus would be someone to pay attention to, but only as one among many, and one whose ideas could be debated along with those of the others. With the second and third options, he is someone we should reject and be done with as soon as possible.[58]

But there is another option, that Jesus is the most important person who ever lived, someone from whom we must not only learn but who is the standard by which to evaluate all other voices. Not only a prophet, but a savior. Yet not only a savior, but *the* Savior in whom we must put our complete faith. This is what the New Testament writers are trying to convince us. That he is the one promised from ancient days, the Messiah that Israel was looking for, the one who has the words of eternal life, the one who was in the beginning with God and was God. The way, the truth, and the life through whom we come to God.

To have faith in Jesus in this sense means receiving the testimony that we find in the New Testament and believing that this is true about Jesus: the testimony of those who compiled and edited the books of Matthew, Mark, Luke, and John; the testimony of those we read about in the book of Acts; the testimony of the other writers, such as the Apostle Paul who first fought against Jesus' followers and then gave his life completely to help others realize and believe that Jesus is Lord. Just as for these witnesses, faith also means trusting Jesus—giving him our ultimate concern—rather than any other savior figure. And it means doing the things that Jesus asks us to do.

Finding a Handle
Embracing a worldview, such as Christianity or anything else, is not a simple matter. Depending on our personality and the ways we have come to engage the world around us, we will find certain elements either more significant or less significant. Most of us will likely expect to see some kind of practical demonstration that something is true. For example, if an ad claims that a certain brand of toothpaste gets teeth whiter, we will expect that our teeth will whiten if we change to that brand.

Many people approach Christianity with that kind of expectation, and to some extent this is consistent with what the Bible offers. "Taste and see that the LORD is good; blessed is the one who takes refuge in him," says the psalmist (Ps. 34:8). "Take my yoke upon you and learn from me," said Jesus, "and you will find rest for your souls" (Matt. 11:29). We are invited to expect results. Yet this does not mean we will find everything just as we anticipate, as we have no doubt learned is true of most relationships.

So how can we be sure that something or someone is true? And how can we be sure that Jesus is the Truth? The simplest answer, perhaps, is that we need to find a "handle," something that clinches the matter for us, at least enough to make a beginning. For many people, the journey of faith has begun with a significant personal experience such as a time when "I knew that God was speaking to me and that I needed to respond." It could be a time recognizing one's sins that needed to be confessed and rejected. I have known personally two atheists who independently were looking at a beautiful natural landscape and who suddenly, to their utter surprise, found themselves talking to God and expressing gratitude for the beauty they were witnessing.

For you it could be one or more of the other three signposts we discussed in chapter 7, or just a fascination with Jesus, all he did, and all he represents. Or the handle might be the growing awareness that all of the reasons and/or excuses for rejecting a belief in God no longer hold any weight. C. S. Lewis reports his own journey from atheism in similar terms, and described himself (at that point) as the most reluctant convert to Christianity in all of England.[59] Whatever your handle, grab onto it and begin the walk of faith. You will have time to explore, refine, test, and sharpen your understanding as you go.

But Is There Really Something That Is True?

Perhaps you have read up to this point and still find yourself dissatisfied. That may be true for *you*, you might be saying, or fine for some religious people, but that doesn't mean it's true for everyone. North Americans live within a culture of tolerated diversity. Everyone of us is exposed to numerous worldview options, some religious and some not. In this way, our situation is much like the cultural context we find reflected in both Old and New Testaments of the Christian Bible.

But there are several ways that such a culture of diversity can go. One is competitive; it says that there may be many options but only one at the most can actually be true or the most true. Another way is the route of Skepticism or Cynicism; this way says that when it comes to the meaning of life, no one can really know whether one of the approaches is most true, objectively speaking; one can only know what seems right for them.

And the latter approach seems to have the upper hand in North American culture at our present time. I mention here only a few of the important factors one must consider when confronted by someone espousing Skepticism or Cynicism (see ch. 2). At the outset, of course, one must wonder at the confidence of those who insist that it is absolutely true that there are no absolute truths! But simplistic aspersions aside, one can sympathize with those for whom the massive amount of worldview options, at least in their subcategory forms, are quite bewildering.

It can easily seem that the human situation is well represented by the story of the blind men and the elephant: each has part of the truth and insists adamantly that the elephant is like a snake, a wall, a fan, and so on. We indeed find persons whose experiences and reflective thinking lead them to adopt very different understandings of the world. We do well to listen to others and learn from their perspectives and understandings.

Yet this approach to life is much too pessimistic. First, we should recognize that relatively few Skeptics and Cynics have ever existed. The vast majority of human beings have believed that the truth about reality actually exists. And most have also believed that it is essentially knowable. Second, let's remember that, with very few exceptions, people in everyday life argue and complain to and against one another in a way that assumes we all agree on what is morally right and wrong (to pick one specific worldview element).

Third, we should notice that if we say, "That's true for you but not for me," we are using the word *true* in a new way. It now means something like "functions effectively" or "serves convincingly" for a person. It no longer means the reality that is above and beyond all of us no matter what we think about it. A bird that flies into a window believes that the window was not there. To say that the nonexistence of the window was "true" for the bird is to talk about perceptions, not truth.

Fourth, to focus on the Skeptic, people who argue assume the validity of argument. They believe that if a premise is true, such as a moral principle (stealing is wrong), and that if a particular action, event, etc., can be shown to be an example of that premise (someone stole something), the conclusion is that it was wrong for that person to steal something. If valid arguments are true, not everything is subjective. Thus, one could consider whether the Skeptic is actually consistent with his or her philosophy. Do they say that there is no objective truth, and yet appeal to it when it fits their needs?[60]

These considerations don't mean that Skepticism or Cynicism must be wrong, but they make it more likely. And if there is objective truth, we can reflect on signposts and testimony, for example, to come in contact with it. Perhaps the deeper issue for many people is that they hunger for truth, yet are discouraged because it seems so hard to find. For such persons, Christians have good news: in Jesus the Truth has come into the world.

Faith in the Midst of Storm

The decision to make a commitment regarding that which is of greatest importance (ultimate concern) has been helpfully described in a kind of weather parable. William James (drawing from Fitz James Stephen) likens our lives to a person stuck in a blinding snowstorm. The wind is howling, the snow brings visibility to almost zero. To remain in such conditions is simply not an option: a person would soon freeze to death. But which way to go? Which path is the right one? One must risk choosing one possible path or another in hope of finding shelter.[61]

As human beings in the midst of life's storm, in a culture that offers little direction or mixed signals, we likewise do not have the luxury of doing nothing. We must decide where we will put our ultimate faith. The point of the parable is not so much that we must rush to a decision, but that a decision must be made and, in fact, we have already done so to some extent. To make that choice wisely means using as much evidence as possible. Fortunately, we have testimony from those who are able to point us to the right path. We thus have good reason to take the necessary risk to find the shelter we so desperately need. We take a step, trusting for more guidance as we go.

In the next chapter, we allow the question of what is true to merge with the question of what is good.

Questions for Reflection and Discussion

1. What reasons are offered by Christianity (or Jesus) for making a faith commitment to Jesus? Are these persuasive for you?

2. What do you think about Jesus? How have you decided to make sense of his life and teachings?

3. What does "soil analysis" mean for you? Are there aspects of your life that seem like rocky or weedy ground?

4. Is there an area of pain and difficulty in your life that remains unresolved? Would you consider wrestling or lamenting about this?

5. Is there something you know about God, either an experience or some other truth, that can be a reference point for faith in the midst of your time of pain or hardship? Are you willing, able, and ready to take the next step, whatever that might be for you?

6. Name something you believe that you learned from a source other than your own experience. How do you determine whether a source is trustworthy or not?

7. Considering the story about choosing which way to go in the midst of a blinding snowstorm, are you pleased with the direction you are traveling? Why or why not?

Suggestions for Further Reading

Martin B. Copenhaver, *Jesus Is the Question*. Nashville, TN: Abingdon, 2014.

Robert Davidson, *The Courage to Doubt: Exploring an Old Testament Theme*. London: SCM, 1983

_____, *Wisdom and Worship*. London: SCM, 1990.

Peter Kreeft, *A Refutation of Moral Relativism: Interviews with an Absolutist*. San Francisco, CA: Ignatius, 1999.

C. S. Lewis, *Mere Christianity*. New York: Macmillan, 1952.

Bob Yoder, *Helping Youth Grieve: The Good News of Biblical Lament*. Eugene, OR: Wipf & Stock, 2015.

CHAPTER 9

Moral Health

Consider the following situation. A young woman bikes to work through a large public park that has attracted many transients. She feels a bit unsafe there but really likes biking through that beautiful area. She consults with a group of friends and considers how she might respond in the event she is attacked. Together they compile the following list of alternatives for how she might deal with such a threat: (1) do nothing; accept that whatever happens is God's will; (2) pray for deliverance but do nothing else; (3) take training for best ways to flee such a situation, e.g., to see possible escape routes, learn to yell loudly; (4) nonlethal defense, e.g., learn martial arts, use Mace; (5) get a gun and train to use it in ways that could result in the attacker's death; and (6) get a gun, be ready to kill the attacker, and then locate his or her family and go kill them. Which of these options would you recommend to the young woman and why?[62]

Evaluating choices in such scenarios is the realm of ethics. Some choices we make are morally neutral, such as deciding which food is your favorite, whether to be a dog or a cat lover, or choosing the color you like best. Moral choices are different. They concern right and wrong, what is holy and what is profane. Is it right to steal? Is it okay to harm another person? Should contracts be honored? Food becomes a moral issue when we ask whether something is poisonous or nutritious, and when we consider how to eat when others are starving.

Ethics, also described as "moral obligation" or "moral duty," is the discipline dealing with such concerns.

Societal Guidance

Societies typically operate with a consensus of what is morally right or wrong, a consensus that guides its members in making the sometimes challenging and costly choices with which they are faced. If you ask someone a question involving moral judgment, they often have an immediate response expressed with conviction, such as, "That's not right!" Or, "No one should get away with that!" Responses like this suggest that they have been nurtured, however indirectly, into a certain understanding of right and wrong. However, to ask them to defend the rationale for their choice is not as easy. It requires a deeper comprehension of ethical decision making.

Our own time is one in which the culture's ethical consensus is being stretched, sometimes to the breaking point. There are also signs that the people of North America, considered as a whole, are decreasing in their ability to wisely engage important ethical challenges. Alasdair MacIntyre began his work *After Virtue* with a fanciful story. He asked his readers to consider an imaginary world in which people had become so upset with the natural sciences that they burned down laboratories, lynched physicists, ravaged libraries, and abolished science teaching in all the schools so that the collective scientific enterprise was no longer functional. All that remained were fragments of articles, books, and research papers, plus a few tools that in time no one knew how to use. Eventually, however, a scientific revival took place and people began to use scientific words and ideas again, terms such as *neutrino* and *specific gravity* and *relativity*. And yet they no longer had the unifying framework for making sense of what was left of the language and concepts of science. In MacIntyre's own words,

> The hypothesis which I wish to advance is that in the actual world which we inhabit the language of morality is in the same state of grave disorder as the language of the natural sciences in the imaginary world which I described. What we

possess, if this view is true, are the fragments of a conceptual scheme, parts which now lack those contexts from which their significance derived. We possess indeed simulacra [representations] of morality, we continue to use many of the key expressions. But we have—very largely, if not entirely—lost our comprehension, both theoretical and practical, of morality.[63]

With similar concern, Christian Smith writes,

American emerging adults are a people deprived, a generation that has been failed, when it comes to moral formation. They have had withheld from them something that every person deserves to have a chance to learn: how to think, speak, and act well on matters of good and bad, right and wrong. Therefore, in Charles Taylor's words, "We have to fight uphill to rediscover the obvious, to counteract the layers of suppression of modern moral consciousness."

Smith urges that people "need to know the moral landscape of the real world that they inhabit. They need some better moral maps and better-equipped guides to show them the way around."[64]

As we look around our culture, we find certain areas of moral agreement, such as consideration for those who are disabled reflected in specially marked prime parking spaces in public lots. On the other hand, we find major disagreement on matters such as the use of money, sexuality, intoxication, how to handle disagreements, and how to respond to violence. It would be easy, simplistic, and ultimately unsatisfying to conclude with the Moral Relativists that each person comes to an understanding of what is right or wrong for themselves, and that morality is a matter of subjective truth that can never be resolved in community-wide agreement. Whether we can agree together on every matter of right and wrong is a challenging question. But the achievability of that goal does not in itself require us to conclude that morality is a matter of subjective truth. We should consider whether a morality exists that is independent of human perception, that can be discovered rather than merely created.

No Real Right and Wrong?

The question of objective morality is a complex one that cannot be adequately addressed here. However, a few points can be raised that may lead us in a helpful direction. Moral Relativists, those who claim that morality is subjective and not independent of each person, notice that individuals and societies disagree about moral issues. Certainly no one would deny that some persons consider abortion immoral while others find it acceptable; some support the death penalty for certain crimes while others urge that it be abolished. Relativists often argue that if we would realize that all morality is subjective, we could eliminate violence in the name of morality. That is, by realizing that we cannot legitimately hold people to a moral standard that they don't accept—because there is no objective standard—we have no grounds for the use of violence to hold people accountable. Further, we would also eliminate the burden of guilt that so many people unnecessarily bear; this is because they allow a standard to be imposed on them by their society or some other group to which they wrongly give power.

The first argument sounds a lot like claiming that it is wrong and harmful to believe that there are things genuinely wrong and harmful. Likewise the second: it is wrong to oppress people by insisting that some things are wrong. Both arguments assume that which they intend to refute. A moral standard is required—a value such as "people should not be harmed"—to find the argument compelling, in which case the arguments undermine themselves.

In addition, can we really believe that moral universals do not exist? Does anyone or any society celebrate a traitor or a rapist? And we praise those who suffer on behalf of others, keep their promises to their own disadvantage, and show respect for their neighbors. That human beings share much agreement with one another is reflected in societal laws and religious codes throughout recorded history. We find respect for the lives and property of others, duties to family members, as well as concern for sexual boundaries, justice, honesty, and the keeping of promises. Such examples suggest the existence of a common or objective standard for considering something to be wrong or right.

Differences and disagreements in these areas seem to concern the details of the issues while agreeing in general about the issue itself. For example, cultures express respect for property in many different ways, but none simply allow a disregard of ownership, however defined.

As for the concern about guilt, it acknowledges a reality most can accept: that human beings have a conscience, something inside that alerts them to actions that are morally right or wrong, either done by themselves or done by others. While guilt may occasionally be misplaced—the result of inappropriate pressure by someone trying to manipulate another—most guilt is an alert that one's own standards have been violated. As a rise in body temperature indicates the need for medical attention, guilt indicates the need for ethical attention.

Just because not everyone's conscience reflects the same moral values is no reason to avoid the more significant factor: that humans experience conscience at all. Evolutionary explanations that such an element in human experience aids in the survival of the fittest do not adequately account for the appearance of such an indicator in an otherwise supposedly materialistic universe.

So we have reason to believe that an objective morality exists. But the differences among us suggest that it is challenging to think and act clearly about such matters. As we conclude this section, it is worth attending to an analogy presented by C. S. Lewis:

> There is a story about a schoolboy who was asked what he thought God was like. He replied that, as far as he could make out, God was "the sort of person who is always snooping around to see if anyone is enjoying himself and then trying to stop it." And I am afraid that is the sort of idea that the word *Morality* raises in a good many people's minds: something that interferes, something that stops you having a good time. In reality, moral rules are directions for running the human machine. Every moral rule is there to prevent a breakdown, or a strain, or a friction, in the running of that machine.[65]

Sources of Ethical Authority

Worldviews have values at their center, and many of these are moral values. The Christian worldview is no different and will be used to illustrate how moral values can be thoughtfully put into practice. The principles described here could presumably be employed with other worldviews.

A variety of reasons could be described and explored to explain why people avoid morally wrong choices and why they choose what is morally right. These reasons might include a bad or a good conscience, fear that bad outcomes (or hope that good outcomes) could occur for one's self or others, God's judgment, God's character and will, pleasing God, or some combination of these. The following discussion will not focus on motivations for making good or bad choices. Rather it will concern how we determine what is right or wrong.

An important consideration when pursuing what is ethical is the question of authority: what sources should be consulted? Christians have typically turned to one or more of the following: conscience, the moral traditions of a church, church leaders, the Bible, and direct divine guidance. Other possible sources include the heritage of one's nation, one's own experience, and the counsel of friends, family, and various persons considered to be wise.

Each of these has merit and some appear in the Bible itself, as we will see in our discussion of Acts 15 below. Scripture is an invaluable source for Christian ethical deliberation partly because it gives us access to the life and truth that Jesus taught and modeled, including his use of the Hebrew Bible (Old Testament). So we will give the Bible special attention.

The study of Scripture takes on a lot of detail. The rabbis counted 613 laws to which they were expected to be faithful, the most famous of which are known as the Ten Commandments. Rabbis also produced summaries in the spirit of Micah 6:8:

> He has shown you, O mortal, what is good.
>   And what does the LORD require of you?
> To act justly and to love mercy
>   and to walk humbly with your God.

Like the rabbis, Jesus summarized the communication from God, referred to as "the law and the prophets," very succinctly, and he did so in two forms. The first is in terms of the two great commandments: to love God supremely with all that we are and to love our neighbor as our self (Matt. 22:36-40).[66] The second summary is known as the Golden Rule: do to others what you wish they would do to you (Matt. 7:12). These summaries help to center Jesus' call and remind us what should motivate our work: to love God and to love other people. This is what God is about and what God calls us to imitate.

Acts 15 as Ethical Model
The account in Acts 15, often referred to as the "Jerusalem Council," is quite helpful for illustrating a Christian perspective on ethical decision making. Here we get to see how followers of Jesus put love of God and love of neighbor into practice regarding a very specific ethical issue. These representatives of Jesus' followers from various locations met in Jerusalem to decide whether non-Jews who were also Jesus' disciples needed to obey all the instructions of Moses or not. Some said yes, others said no. The issues were fundamental and complex. The instruction to circumcise males went back to Abraham and was affirmed by Moses. Jesus was himself circumcised, and in all his teaching the only time he mentions circumcision he does so positively. Certainly he did not abolish it (Luke 2:21; John 7:22-23). Yet amazingly the group in Jerusalem deliberated together and agreed that circumcision was not necessary for Gentiles.

Several important elements in ethical deliberation are illustrated in this report, the first four of which were later designated the Wesleyan Quadrilateral (from Christian leader John Wesley) or the Hermeneutical Spiral.[67] First, we see that *Scripture* was taken very seriously—Moses was cited as was the prophet Isaiah—and, second, their *tradition* on the issue is evaluated (vv. 16-18). Third, the *experience* of those reporting was taken into account as a possible indicator of God's work among them (v. 12). Fourth, the group used *reason* and *reflection* as they argued with each other (vv. 5-21). Fifth, when they came to agreement, they *wrote* out their conclusions for sharing with others (vv. 22-29). Finally, we should consider that it was a group working together on this issue and the makeup of the group. No one played a role more privileged than the rest, though James proposed a solution (vv. 13-21). In sum, this was a *group of leaders*, persons chosen as qualified to represent larger bodies of believers, entrusted to deliberate together to seek the mind of God on this important matter.

Discerning Right from Wrong

Keeping in mind the elements in Acts 15 noted above, we will now briefly review past Christian practice. In the history of ethics, four classical approaches have been adopted for determining right or wrong, and each, by itself, has significant shortcomings.[68]

Situation Ethics. This approach emphasizes the uniqueness of the situation in which decisions need to be made. Adherents emphasize that each situation has its own distinctive elements that cannot be appraised except in that situation. Proponents have typically advocated for unconditional love as the prime—or only—moral value to which they seek to comply as they decide what to do. Joseph Fletcher developed a version of this ethical system, supported by several strategic principles, such as, anything besides love is good only as it contributes to love; the end (outcome) determines whether something is loving or not; the end justifies the means used to accomplish it; the end is evaluated based on the potential good to be accomplished in pragmatic terms; and the goal is the greatest good for the greatest number. Traditional ethical values such as honesty and respect for property are relevant only if they are consistent with love in a particular set of circumstances. Key biblical texts include Mark 12:28-31 (the love commands), 1 Corinthians 13:13 (the greatest is love), and 1 John 4:7-12 (God is love).

If a person walking ahead of you on the sidewalk dropped a bag of groceries, you might determine that the loving thing in that moment would be to stop and help the person gather their food items. Respect for property would be relevant in that situation, but not if you needed to risk the groceries to push the person out of the way of a car headed for the sidewalk. On the other hand, if a family was walking ahead of you on the sidewalk and one of the children began to rip flowers out of a neighbor's flower bed, yet the parents insisted that you do nothing to intervene because the child's problem was medically-related, the situation and the possibility of expressing love would become more complex—including whether property should be respected.

Important concerns about situation ethics include whether likely outcomes can accurately be determined, whether there are other principles besides love that should be ethically valued, whether people need rules to avoid sin, and how to safeguard the concerns of those in the minority when the goal is the greatest good for the greatest number.

Legalism. A second approach employs rules that reflect a variety of important moral values. The assumption is that rules can cover every ethical situation. A biblical example of important rules would be the Ten Commandments (Exod. 20:1-17), most of which were specifically reaffirmed by Jesus. If one were to notice money fall out of someone's purse or briefcase, one might immediately review the rule, "You shall not steal." Putting it into action could involve drawing the person's attention to the money rather than keeping it for oneself.

On the other hand, if you were in Germany during the Second World War hiding several Jews in a secret room upstairs in your house, and a uniformed German officer knocked on the door and asked you directly whether any Jews were in the house, the situation would become more complicated. Again, using the Ten Commandments, "You shall not give false testimony" indicates that honesty is an important value, while another admonishes you not to kill. Yet you know if you honestly answer the question, the Jews would almost certainly be harmed or killed in a Nazi concentration camp. The key question is what to do when moral rules conflict.

Principlism. This approach seeks to compensate for some of the complications with a legalist approach. Principles are more general than rules and help to mediate conflicts between rules. In the Nazi situation described in the previous paragraph, one might have a principle of honesty and a principle of benevolence, and a third principle that says benevolence ranks higher than honesty.

On the other hand, it may not be possible to establish a guideline between all principles so that one is always higher than the other. For example, the principle of benevolence might conflict with the principle of justice. Sometimes it seems that justice should win out and other times it may seem that benevolent compassion is the most appropriate. This is the kind of situation where the ethical question must take into account the broader beliefs, values, and narrative of one's worldview and suggests a fourth approach. Another problem with principlism is that we may be tempted to avoid a direct command of Jesus by our definition of principles. Jesus told us not to let others know when we give gifts to the poor (Matt. 6:1), but we might avoid that through a principle of expressing gratitude.

Contextualism and Narrative Ethics. More recently, an approach to ethics has arisen that pays more attention to the communal nature of ethical decision making. Adherents emphasize that rules and principles get their meaning from the various contexts in which they are understood. They say that not only is it the case (descriptively) that people tend to be loyal to the values and perspectives of the communities in which they find themselves (family, nation, etc.), but in fact Christian ethics (prescriptively) *should* be done in the context of a living faith community and in connection with the narrative of God's people reflected in the Bible. In case of conflict, the faith community and its understandings should overrule the perspectives of the other communities of which the person is part.

Like each of the other three classic approaches to Christian ethics, this one has a complication, yet this weakness can be found in the other three as well: the challenge for Christians to come to agreement as they engage the core of their worldview understandings in connection with ethical questions. An illustration of such disagreements will be provided in the following section.

A Four-Level Process of Moral Deliberation

It is time now to consider these four approaches and see if there is a better way forward. Ethicists Glen Stassen and David Gushee argue, first, that each of these approaches by itself has serious deficiencies for achieving satisfactory answers to ethical questions, as indicated in the summary above. Second, they insist that all four levels of ethical deliberation are illustrated in the Bible and have something important to contribute. Finally, they propose a process by which each of these levels is respected in interaction with the others: specific circumstances are taken into account, rules are supported by principles, and principles are connected to the basic convictions of Christian faith in the process of making ethical decisions. They employ their model out of a self-consciously Christian worldview and privilege the instruction and practice of Jesus. Yet the basic concept of the model could also be employed with other worldviews.

To illustrate the Stassen-Gushee model, we will consider the issue of capital punishment, whether or not a person's life should be ended as punishment for crimes such as murder. The following discussion is summarized in the accompanying chart where two Christian arguments concerning capital punishment are summarized. Notice how each level corresponds to one of the historic ways of doing ethics described in the previous section.

Basic convictions are the deepest level of conviction, those beliefs that concern the nature and character of God, of Jesus Christ, of human beings, of the rest of creation, and concerning what God has done and is doing in the world. Explanations for basic convictions are typically found in biblical or theological statements concerning those subjects as well as narratives, notably in the Bible, that illustrate them. On the subject of capital punishment, we could begin with a statement of human distinction from the rest of creation—humans are created in God's image (Gen. 1:27)—and a statement of God's nature—God is responsible for vengeance and is alone qualified to judge (Gen. 18:25; Ps. 82:8). These are basic Christian convictions about humans and God that are relevant to our issue. We note that at this point Argument 1 agrees with Argument 2.

We come now to *principles*, which are rooted in the basic convictions and provide support and critique for rules. Here we could provide a statement of human value: human life is of eternal worth, established in God's love and desire to save people (Isa. 45:22; John 3:16). We find our first divergence in the two arguments with the second principle focused on God: the First Argument emphasizes that God delegates responsibility to carry out judgment, a conclusion that is sometimes connected to Romans 13:4. The Second Argument emphasizes a principle also found in Scripture: God alone has the right to carry out vengeance and take life (Gen. 50:19; Deut. 32:35/ Rom. 12:19). Jesus' principle to love one's enemy could be considered. The divergent outcomes on capital punishment are thus traceable to the principles level.

Rules tell directly what to do or not to do. The First Argument interprets Genesis 9:6 as a rule that calls for capital punishment as the consequence for murder. It understands the sixth of the Ten Commandments to prohibit *murder* rather than human killing of any kind (Exod. 20:13). The Second Argument understands the sixth commandment to prohibit humans from *any* killing, even if society-sanctioned in capital punishment or war. Thus it is translated "You shall not *kill*," and a rule that prohibits capital punishment can be constructed on that basis.

Finally, the *particular judgment* level is the place at which a specific action is indicated. For Argument 1, that could include efforts to support capital punishment laws in one's society, and it might be reflected in the choice of someone who takes a job as an executioner in the justice system. Actions for Argument 2 might include efforts to eliminate capital punishment laws, and the choice of someone to avoid the role of executioner in favor of the health profession.

Three points need to be made about the use of this process. First, this is especially insightful for the use of Scripture in ethics, but as mentioned previously, other sources of ethical insight are also important. Second, the context in which Scripture interpretation and ethical deliberation take place for the Christian is in the believing community. Third, Stassen and Gushee rightly privilege the life and teachings of Jesus for

Christian ethics; the extent to which Jesus is engaged is evident in the deliberation by which a Christian group reaches the conclusion of either Argument 1 or Argument 2 in the capital punishment example reflected in the following chart.

	Argument 1	Argument 2
Particular Judgments: This is what people would actually do about the topic for each of the Arguments	Defend capital punishment if administered fairly within a justice system	Seek to abolish the death penalty from the justice system
Rules: Statements that apply to all similar cases, tell directly what to do or not do	* You shall not murder (Exod. 20:13) * Anyone who murders another shall be put to death	* You shall not kill (Exod. 20:13) * Do not practice capital punishment for crimes
Principles: Support rules or criticize them; more general than rules, does not tell directly what to do	* Human life is of eternal worth * God delegates responsibility to carry out judgment	* Human life is of eternal worth * God reserves the right to carry out vengeance and death * Jesus: love your enemies
Basic Convictions: Core theological beliefs that make up a Christian worldview	* Humans are created in God's image * God is responsible for vengeance and is alone qualified to judge	* Humans are created in God's image * God is responsible for vengeance and is alone qualified to judge

Three Spheres of Ethics

In conclusion, C. S. Lewis has provided an interesting analogy for the three realms in which ethics operates. He asks us to consider human beings like a fleet of ships sailing in formation.

> The voyage will be a success only, in the first place, if the ships do not collide and get in one another's way; and, secondly, if each ship is seaworthy and has her engines in good

order. As a matter of fact, you cannot have either of these two things without the other. If the ships keep on having collisions they will not remain seaworthy very long. On the other hand, if their steering gears are out of order they will not be able to avoid collisions.[69]

We tend to think of ethics mainly in regard to ships getting in each other's way. And that is largely what the four-level model is about: discerning what practices are best for a living and loving society of people in right relation (Christians say) with God. But the ship analogy helps us realize that our internal functioning is also important. We will address the matter of internal functioning, called *virtues*, in this book's final chapter.[70]

Lewis also highlighted a third dimension of ethics using the same ship analogy: the ships' destination. He notes that "however well the fleet sailed, its voyage would be a failure if it were meant to reach New York and actually arrived at Calcutta":

Morality, then, seems to be concerned with three things. Firstly, with fair play and harmony between individuals. Secondly, with what might be called tidying up or harmonising the things inside each individual. Thirdly, with the general purpose of human life as a whole: what man was made for: what course the whole fleet ought to be on . . . .[71]

Worldviews, as we have seen, carry a vision of the final goal or purpose of humanity. Lewis's summary thus nicely aligns with our concern for worldview, ethics, and virtues in connection with vocation.

Questions for Reflection and Discussion

1. Do you believe that there is an objective right and wrong that all should seek to agree on? What problems are there if we cannot agree?

2. What moral principles, if any, do you believe are something absolutely good or absolutely bad? What would you say to someone who disagreed with you about them?
3. In what ways do you find the Stassen-Gushee model helpful? What parts are still unclear?
4. Do you agree that North American culture has not adequately educated its members in appropriate ways of discerning and practicing ethical behavior? What evidence can you give for your answer?
5. What are the three spheres of ethics? Which is of most interest to you? Which do you think is most urgent for our time?

Suggestions for Further Reading

Richard B. Hays, *The Moral Vision of the New Testament: Community, Cross, New Creation*. San Francisco, CA: HarperSanFrancisco, 1996.

Joseph J. Kotva, *The Christian Case for Virtue Ethics*. Washington, DC: Georgetown University Press, 1997.

C. S. Lewis, Book 3, "Christian Behaviour," in *Mere Christianity*. New York: Macmillan, 1952.

Glen H. Stassen and David P. Gushee, *Kingdom Ethics: Following Jesus in Contemporary Context*, 2nd ed. Grand Rapids, MI: Eerdmans, 2016.

CHAPTER 10

A Vision of the Good Life

Previously we have reflected on the significance of world-views as a lens by which we interpret what is around us. The values of a worldview are sometimes described as its vision of the "good life," the goal and purpose of human existence. This chapter explores the film *Pleasantville*, a hidden gem of a Postmodern parable on what constitutes the good life for a society. Through careful critique, it has potential to help us understand God's *shalom* vision for life together.

Pleasantville

In *Pleasantville* (written and directed by Gary Ross), two American teenagers (played by Tobey Maguire and Reese Witherspoon) are sucked into their television set and end up living in a 1950s sitcom. *Pleasantville* opens in 1990s America, which comes across as rude, decadent, and dangerous. A teenager named David languishes in front of the tube, watching a rerun of a 1950s sitcom named "Pleasantville" (similar to "Father Knows Best"), in which everybody is always wholesome and happy. Meanwhile, his mother squabbles with her ex-husband, and his trampy sister Jennifer prepares for a hot date. While David and Jennifer are fighting over the remote control, they break the remote. Just then, there's a knock at the door and a friendly TV repairman (Don Knotts) offers them a device "with more oomph."[72]

They click it, and magically they're both in Pleasantville, a black-and-white world of picket fences and bobby socks, where it never rains, there is no art, all the books in the library are blank, where everybody is white and middle class, has a job, couples sleep in twin beds, no one ever uses the toilet, and everyone follows the same cheerful script. Life always goes according to plan, and during basketball practice every shot goes in.

David and Jennifer become Bud and Mary Sue Parker in Pleasantville and slowly introduce change to the town. Bud is frustrated at the mindlessness of the citizens, Mary Sue is frustrated at their sexlessness. As a result, here and there a few things—and eventually a few people—begin to turn from black and white to color. At first it seems that sexual experience is what triggers the change, but eventually it becomes clear that the issue encompasses more than that: color comes to people when they get in touch with their inner self and their inner feelings, some pleasantly and some not so pleasantly.

The changes result in Bud and Mary Sue's TV mother Betty (Joan Allen) leaving her husband George (William H. Macy) to spend time with Bill Johnson (Jeff Daniels), who runs the local soda fountain, and other women also start questioning their roles. Soon the (male) town council is up in arms and passes laws in an attempt to stop the changes. The prejudice and fear against "coloreds" connects easily to similar terms used in racist America.

After going on an artistic painting spree, Bud and Bill are brought to trial. Those in color sit in the balcony while the mayor holds the accused accountable for disturbing the pleasantness of the town. During the exchange, Bud argues that what is inside people needs to come out and that it cannot be stopped. The mayor, in his angry rebuttal, changes from black and white to color; when he sees his reflection in a mirror, he flees the courtroom. As a result, the whole town turns into brilliant and spectacular color. In the process of their sitcom experience, Jennifer realizes that she has moved on from her obsession with sex to a desire to learn and grow as a person. David, upon returning to the 1990s, is able to counsel his mother that there is no perfect house, car, or life. Rather, it is what we make it to be.

Assessing the Parable

Philosopher Nicholas Wolterstorff proposes a major clash among worldviews on the basis of what constitutes the good life. The Enlightenment organizing concept (connected with a Naturalist/Materialist worldview) is *freedom*, while *order* is the concept traceable to Plato.[73] *Pleasantville* illustrates the tensions between the two, with the former championed by such writers as Mark Twain and D. H. Lawrence, and the latter identified with Christianity (at least 1950s style). The attempt to maintain order as the highest good denies too much of true humanity, the film suggests. Even though freedom as the highest good turns loose all kinds of scary emotions, it offers more potential for healthy living, says the film.

The film represents the lack of realism in the "order" worldview in a variety of ways: bathrooms in the soda shop without toilets (symbolic of a subject never acknowledged), streets that go nowhere (symbolic of no world beyond their tiny region),[74] firefighters who don't know about fire (symbolic of a world without tragedy), no rain (no difficulties). More significantly, the film takes on the abuses of the 1950s, notably the lack of respect for women, for the arts, and for non-Caucasian persons. For such reasons, critic Roger Ebert praised *Pleasantville*:

> The film observes that sometimes pleasant people are pleasant simply because they have never, ever been challenged. That it's scary and dangerous to learn new ways . . . . *Pleasantville* is the kind of parable that encourages us to re-evaluate the good old days and take a fresh look at the new world we so easily dismiss as decadent. Yes, we have more problems. But also more solutions, more opportunities and more freedom. I grew up in the '50s. It was a lot more like the world of *Pleasantville* than you might imagine. Yes, my house had a picket fence, and dinner was always on the table at a quarter to six, but things were wrong that I didn't even know the words for.

The film proposes "freedom" as the better of the two alternatives, and knowledge (note the role of books) as the means of salvation. However, it never suggests how certain perennial issues might be addressed. Here are two of them.

Morality and Spontaneity. There is a tension between true and permanent moral value realities and the spontaneity humans can and should exercise within those constraints. This arises out of the ways in which human beings, from the dawn of recorded history, have sought to both affirm the good impulses and regulate the destructive impulses we find within ourselves. An important example is found in the film: limits on artistic freedom, e.g., what about Internet child pornography; recently the U.S. courts refused to allow prosecution on the grounds that proposed legislation did not distinguish between pornography and art.

Individuality and Community. The film also does not offer a way to handle the tension between communal mores and individual freedoms. We are left with the assumption that if people will simply become uninhibited and exercise what is inside them—both good and bad—things will get along much better (although acknowledging vaguely that there will be problems and danger). Perhaps most significantly, the Enlightenment's freedom concept is inadequate because it is based, not on a positive idea, but upon rejecting other ideas. It begs the question, "Freedom for what?"

Criticizing a Christian Worldview

Most significant for our present discussion is the way the Bible's vision of the good life is represented in the film: as aligned with the "order" concept and the problems associated with it. Biblical symbolism is evident in several cases. Bud's girlfriend offers him an apple (followed by lightning and thunder), which we later see that he has eaten, reminiscent of the woman and man eating forbidden fruit in the Garden of Eden (Gen. 3). Everyone is fearful when it rains, reminiscent of the judgment of rain and flood (Gen. 6–9), but Bud calms them by saying it is "just rain," and revels in it. Even more significant is the role of the TV repairman. He serves as a kind of deity figure, transcendent of both the 1990s and Pleasantville, transporting the nineties teens into the sitcom world and choosing when to retrieve them from it. He criticizes Bud for eating the apple and for stirring up change in Pleasantville, but then we discover he really wishes for Bud and Mary Sue to do what he is telling them *not* to do; this suggests that God gave human beings commands so that they could grow into mature creatures by disobeying them. The film implies that there can be no true and healthy individuality that chooses only good and not evil. In fact, the film suggests that the concept of good and evil is part of the biblical/Platonic/order worldview that is so harsh and crippling to human existence.

Is it okay for Betty to leave her husband George and be with Bill? In a concluding scene, we find the three of them sitting together on a bench. They don't know what they will freely choose next, but in deciding, they are responsible for the reality that they create. Thus, the film offers a version of Existentialism in its advocacy for freedom. This is evident as well in David's concluding conversation with his mother: there is no perfect house, no perfect life, and apparently no perfect morality. Life is what you decide it should be.

Freedom, Order, and Shalom

The film *Pleasantville* presents two central worldview values—order and freedom—and urges us to choose the latter. It sets up this contest of values by first acknowledging the brokenness of the 1990s world, and we see, for example, the longing David has for a world in which parents stay together and care for their children, as well as the shallow sensuality of Jennifer. We are tempted, the film suggests, to want to return to those earlier times in this country where family and friendship were more stable. But not so fast. Taking a closer look, we find that those days had their own problems. In fact, if we could just let go of the legacy of that ordered world—concepts such as the perfect house and perfect life—we could get on with using our freedom to produce a better world. Thus, in the process, the film also urges us to reject biblical faith, which it associates with order, the problems of the 1950s, and the nagging hold-over problems still plaguing the 1990s.

Hopefully, followers of Jesus will not be too defensive when legitimate criticism is directed at those claiming to be Christians: specifically, those who have abused others, whether by gender, in the arts, or according to race. Christians should know better and must do better. It is an equally legitimate challenge, however, to address the question, "Does the film rightly label 'biblical' the approach to order that it rejects?"

Let us consider that the answer to this question is negative. Not only is a biblical worldview wrongly identified with the view of order presented in the film, but the alternative likewise fails to appreciate where it does and does not align with the Bible's vision.

For purposes of this discussion, the biblical vision of the good life will be represented by the Hebrew term *shalom*. This term, often translated by the word *peace*, embodies a rich and complex concept not easily conveyed in English. While the word *peace* suggests primarily the absence of conflict, *shalom* represents the presence of such things as good relationships, success, good health, interconnectedness, and justice.[75] When understood correctly, it provides a third option between *Pleasantville*'s presentations of order and freedom. Wolterstorff labels this third organizing concept "happiness," and traces it to Aristotle.[76]

In fact, no philosophical, theological, or political vision is sustainable unless it offers a way to navigate both order and freedom, as well as the two other related pairs mentioned above: morality vs. spontaneity and individuality vs. commu-nity. To put it succinctly, *shalom* affirms both order and freedom, but not in the ways seen in the film. The freedom promoted by the film is primarily a lack of restraint. It means no laws that restrict artistic expression, no moral codes that restrain sexual expression, and no social mores that inhibit the exploration of whatever one finds inside oneself. Order is the opposite of those things: it is the restriction that comes through law, moral codes, and social constraint. The film does not begin to address how the tensions between the freedom of two groups or two people would be accommodated, nor how those things considered destructive would be restrained.

The film has no proposal for how the consensus of morality, expressed over many millennia and across many cultures, would be embraced and nurtured. This is where Christian faith, though in some senses traditional, is more radical and more helpful. For Christian faith, *freedom* means the ability to do what is good and life-giving, not doing simply what a person happens to want to do (John 8:31-36; 1 Cor. 10:23-24; Gal. 5:13-15). So it offers standards by which what is healthy for both the individual and the group can be established. This includes respect for those who are different from the majority, affirmation of artistic expression, and appreciation for the place of women in society (Exod. 12:49; 22:21; 26:1, 36; Rom. 16:1-7; Gal. 3:28).

Order in Christian faith means organizing the world in ways that serve others, not simply the power to control others for the benefit of one person or their group. It provides a context in which abuse and neglect can be addressed and affirms the morality to which the oppressed can appeal for compensation (Exod. 20; 2 Kings 8:1-6).

Thus, Christian faith in *shalom* finds a place for both order and freedom in the context of accountability to God who embodies these attributes and wove them into the universe made in the divine image.

A Vision of Shalom
What might a shalom vision for the good life look like? We noted the stories of Le Chambon and Timisoara in chapter 6, communities who showed evidence of God's shalom vision among them. One dramatic presentation with shalom elements is the film *Places in the Heart* (1984). Set in the U.S. South in 1935, with weather and economic challenges that characterized the Great Depression, Edna Spalding's husband is killed by a drunken gunman. As she struggles to keep farm and family intact, the story reflects not only the hardships of the era but also its bigotry and racism.

A shalom community is formed by this poor white woman (Sally Field) and her two children, an out-of-work black man (Danny Glover) who has the skills to plant and tend her crops, and a blind boarder (John Malkovich) who proves more resourceful than expected. Meanwhile we learn of distresses of a more nonvirtuous kind in the lives of others in the community: greed, unfaithfulness, the KKK. The film's last scene is perhaps as ambiguous as it is hopeful. Nevertheless, we see a glimpse of God's shalom vision as all the characters in the film—friends and enemies, wives and mistresses, living and dead, black and white—in the midst of worship, take communion together in the local church. This scene brings together God's work of reconciliation, not only for the ultimate future but also among people here and now.

In fact, that is how God's shalom vision works itself out. It is not a matter of tearing down the structures of a society and starting over to build an ideal society. Rather it is like planting mustard seeds or working leaven into dough. It maneuvers slowly to accomplish God's purposes, to transform people and structures.

From this general understanding, we now need to ask how those operating from a Christian worldview might interact with those around them who do not share that worldview. As we review six models used by Christians through the centuries, keep looking for indications of shalom vision or its absence.

Questions for Reflection and Discussion

1. Evaluate the three options presented by *Pleasantville* and its critique in this chapter: order, freedom, *shalom*. Which do you prefer and why?
2. What is your personal vision of the "good life"? What role do you play in making it happen?
3. Can God's shalom vision for people occur in this time as well as in the ultimate future? Why or why not?
4. Challenge Bud's claim in *Pleasantville* that you can't stop what's inside you from coming out. Consider the text,

"(let) all that is within me, bless (the LORD's) holy name" (Ps. 103:1b NRSV). Might this require us to evaluate what's inside, to sort between those aspects of life that give praise to God and those that do not? How is this similar to the need of all cultures and communities to honor what is good and restrict and control that which is bad?

Suggestions for Further Reading

Nicholas Wolterstorff, *Until Justice and Peace Embrace*. Grand Rapids, MI: Eerdmans, 1983.

Perry B. Yoder, *Shalom: The Bible's Word for Salvation, Justice, and Peace*. Newton, KS: Faith and Life, 1987.

CHAPTER 11

Engaging Culture

As I write these words, the politico-ideological movement known by such acronyms as ISIS and ISIL is capturing the attention, and sometimes the imagination, of the world by its attempts to carve out a new political entity. Their vision is different than those of Western secular democracies, Communist countries, and present Islamic states. In 1995, well before the 9/11 attacks on New York and Washington, DC, in 2001, Benjamin Barber published a book that became a *New York Times* bestseller titled *Jihad vs. McWorld*. The book demonstrates how two ideological forces have been battling for supremacy on the world stage. In Barber's presentation, *McWorld* stands for "free-market institutions," "commercialized and ambitiously secularist materialism," and "integrative modernization and aggressive economic and cultural globalization," while *Jihad*, including groups like ISIS/ISIL, is a Muslim form of "disintegral tribalism and reactionary fundamentalism."[77]

Though the title of the book may imply that one must, in the midst of this epic struggle, choose one or the other of these two options, Barber demonstrates in some post-9/11 reflections that the situation is not that simple. One of his main concerns is that democracy might be lost in the midst of the battle, since each side "for its own reasons seems indifferent to freedom's fate." He urges that democracy be "the instrument by which the world avoids the stark choice between a sterile cultural

monism (McWorld) and a raging cultural fundamentalism
(Jihad), neither of which services diversity or civic liberty."

In his comments on America's response to 9/11, he
particularly cites the importance of justice, insisting that justice
"will remain appropriate only if the compass of its meaning is
extended from retributive to distributive justice."[78] That is,
Barber realizes that both of these approaches constitute serious
danger for inhabitants of the earth. To make a better world will
require not only a third way, but this third way will need to
focus on justice that cares about a fair distribution of resources
more than it cares about assigning blame and punishing some
group of people.

Tom Sine, in his reflection on Barber's analysis of these two
forces (globalization and fragmentation), urges that there is "a
third force at work in human society that isn't apparent to
those outside the community of faith: the Creator God who
passionately loves a people and a world and is working
through the subversion of the mustard seed to make all things
new."[79] As Sine wrote in an earlier book, he believes that "God
has chosen to change the world through the lowly, the unas-
suming and the imperceptible," and he cites Jesus' mustard
seed parable as confirmation (Mark 4:30-32; Matt. 13:31-32; cf.
17:20).[80] From Sine's perspective, the three approaches can be
compared as shown on the chart below.[81]

Thus, Sine argues that God's primary strategy in the world
operates differently than the methodologies of either of these
two other forces. In the discussion below, we will consider
three other approaches as well. Six ways of relating to culture
may be a helpful start in wading through the diversity of our
increasingly Pluralistic cultures, not only in the West but also
elsewhere in the world. One can hardly speak meaningfully of
the "culture" of the United States, whether geographically
(Northeast, West, etc.) or in regard to the multiple subcultures
within a given region. We will consider some recently published studies, which themselves draw on more thorough explorations, both anthropological and theological.[82] It will be
helpful to notice how Christians in particular have related to
the bigger world in various contexts and circumstances.

AGENDAS IN CONFLICT	McWorld	Jihad	Mustard Seed
Defining the ultimate	Defines the ultimate in terms of economic growth and efficiency	Secure territory controlled by members of the ideology	Spiritual and societal transformation to God's ways and goals
Image of the better future	Western progress, the American Dream, and individual economic upscaling	Undercut the power of opposing political entities	A world transformed so that all can experience God's blessings
Agent of change	Human initiative through technological, economic and political power, supported by violence	Violent power, terrorism, crusade, no compromise with the opposition	God's initiative through the small, the insignificant, the mustard seed without use of forceful violence
Primary values	Individualism, consumerism, and materialism	Moral absolutes, communal prosperity, radical commitment	Community, spirituality, and radical faith

The present discussion builds on chapter 6, which emphasized the essential place of God's people in the divine plan for the world. Here, in the context of the culture clashes of our present era, we will seek some historical perspective on how Christians over the past two millennia have engaged (or failed to engage) the culture around them. It needs to be noted at the outset that in some ways it is artificial to think that we can engage culture uniformly. As Joseph Kotva put it, the

> issue is not whether to participate in broader culture and society, but how and when. . . . The individual or community may object to and refuse to participate in specific aspects of the larger culture . . . it can entail a discerning and selective engagement.[83]

So this catalog of six models will be a bit slippery. It is artificial to think that each person or group operates consistently within only one of the "Christ and Culture" categories.

We do well to consider in addition the plight of many who live today in contexts of serious oppression, ideological, political, and physical. As D. A. Carson notes,

> choices of entire paradigms as to what we think the relationship between Christ and culture *ought* to be—or, more narrowly, what the relationship between the church and the state ought to be—is a luxury reserved for those who have options. Those of us who live in relative security must learn this lesson in humility.[84]

Yet given such cautions, the challenge of these options is to consider which of them may be closest to God's intentions for people to live out their calling in our time and place.

Christ and Culture

In 1951, theologian H. Richard Niebuhr (brother of theologian Reinhold Niebuhr) published *Christ and Culture*, a survey of Christian perspectives on how believers have related to those around them. For Niebuhr, *culture* involves the changes that human beings impose on the created world, e.g., government, economy, family, art, entertainment, language, customs. It is always social, it concerns human achievement, it embraces values, and it involves purposes and goals that are intended to be good for human beings in the world here and now. By *Christ* he means the life and the radical demands of Jesus, including exhortations that people should love their neighbors and enemies, trust God to provide for their needs, and love God more than concerns of this world.[85]

The purpose of the book is to assess the way Christian people have lived out the connection between Christ and culture. In short, if Jesus is Lord of the cosmos, as Christians declare (Rom. 10:9; 1 Cor. 12:3), how do his followers relate in a variety of ways to the society in which they find themselves and, in particular, to its government? In terms we have examined previously, what does it mean to be a member of

God's family as well as a member of our sociological one; to have identity as part of God's "people" and also as part of one's ethnic group; to be a citizen of God's kingdom yet also a citizen of our local kingdom? As he addresses this problem through historical study, he develops a taxonomy of categories or models.

This chapter is included to help readers understand and consider the ways they engage, or would like to engage, those with whom they live and interact in broader society. Depending on your own commitment, "Christ" in our present discussion can stand for the heart of your worldview, the values and perspectives that you hold. And depending on the nature of that worldview and the organization of your society, you may encounter or perceive either more or less tension between your worldview and that society.

Here are six possible ways you and those who believe like you might relate to the surrounding world. For this presentation, I have often given new labels to Niebuhr's categories, and I have taken the liberty of adding a sixth category to his original five. (Later in this chapter there are some ideas for adapting these six to a nonbiblical worldview.)

1. Capitulating. According to Niebuhr, one approach (that he calls "Christ of Culture") is to minimize the tension between Christ and the surrounding culture, to harmonize by removing some of his teachings. In the history of Christianity, Niebuhr places Gnostic groups among the examples of this type, who chose selectively from both Christ and the culture. He also cites Abélard, John Locke, Immanuel Kant, nineteenth and twentieth century liberalism, and Thomas Jefferson, who sought to correct some of Christ's teachings on the grounds of both their later corruption in transmission and their faulty original pronouncements. Within the Bible, the Sadducees may be the prime example. From what we know of them, they seemed eager to depreciate whatever of their faith was necessary in order to retain as much political power as the representatives of Rome would allow them.[86]

The insight of this approach comes in two ways: the importance and value of joining with others for common goals, and the humility necessary to recognize that others may know things that can be beneficial for us. Note John 1:9, for example, which indicates that the true Light enlightens all people. The risk or danger of this approach, and the reason "capitulating" is an appropriate label, is because it has so little confidence in the convictions of its own adopted worldview. Niebuhr suspects that "Christ" for this approach is really a chameleon: it simply takes on whatever values and characteristics are attached to that symbol by the worldview that is borrowing it.

A current example of those from within a historically Christian tradition who take this position is Episcopal bishop John Shelby Spong. He argues that Christians should emphasize love and see Jesus as an ideal human being, but rejects Christian teaching about sin, judgment, and the importance of salvation, which he considers archaic and unhelpful.[87] Yet these are some of the core understandings that distinguish Christianity from other worldviews. Concisely put, this model employs a worldview for a goal or value that exists outside that worldview, though possibly compatible with it. In the case of Christianity, it employs the teachings of Christ and/or the Bible as a means to accomplish some objectives distinct from what is found there. Christ is made to align with a social value not discernible from the words of the Gospels.

2. Synthesizing. This model ("Christ above Culture") embraces Christian teaching and the Bible but believes they are insufficient without also drawing upon important teachings that come from other sources. The insight of this approach is that all truth is God's truth, and that God communicates to people through a variety of channels. The heavens tell the glory of God (Ps. 19:1-2; Matt. 2:1-12), and God can speak through a pagan prophet and his donkey (Num. 22), pagan kings (Gen. 14:18-20; 20:9-10), and a pagan priest (Exod. 18).

This model is adopted especially by those who wish to use political and other forms of power to fight those considered evil and to establish a strong, godly culture. Historical examples include Clement of Alexandria, Justin Martyr, the Roman Emperor Constantine, Thomas Aquinas, and those involved with the Crusades to the Holy Land. Aquinas is the model example, who sought to synthesize the ethics of culture (drawn significantly from the ancient Greeks) with the ethics of the gospel, and likewise with law. This approach (also called "politicizing") shows up today in political movements that claim they are the true embodiment of Christian faith, and that all true Christians should join them.

The insight of this approach is that wherever believers find themselves, they will need to draw on the best wisdom that their culture can offer in order to live out their faithfulness. This is because the Bible simply does not address every aspect of life. Or at least it does not address it in ways that can be transferred simplistically through time and geography to other locations. When we consider this along with the evidence that especially Old Testament believers were drawing on the cultures around them in the process of living out God's directives to them, there is precedent for further synthesis of this sort.[88] Politically, we can note Israel's wars of conquest (destroying or driving out local pagans); kings during the period of the monarchy, such as Solomon, who allowed syncretism between Yahwism and the worship of pagan deities; and perhaps also Zealots during the time of Jesus.

Niebuhr criticized this approach for failing adequately to appreciate human sinfulness in the cultural dimensions to be joined with the teachings of Christ. An additional complication in our own era is an increasing lack of cultural consensus with which to engage. Historically, this model has been associated with the two-level distortion of vocation: those in religious professions are at the top level, all others at the (tolerated) lower level (ch. 12); but it is not clear that this would be necessary.

3. Privatizing. This model ("Christ and Culture in Paradox") traces its roots to Martin Luther and his version of the Protestant Reformation in sixteenth-century Europe. Its insight is that each person is accountable for their response to God's call. Luther's understanding is significantly grounded in his

German context and the confidence he held with the professional "stations" within it. Luther believed that any station in which it was possible to function honestly represented a divine calling. He thus rejected the two-level distortion of vocation but was vulnerable to the equal-level distortion: for each person any work is acceptable (see ch. 12). Honest stations included roles in the family, in the economic arena, and in political life. He did not anticipate much movement of persons from one station to another, an approach that aligned with some words of the Apostle Paul (1 Cor. 7:20). Rather, the stations were largely passed down to succeeding generations, and each had its known values and respected morality.

Niebuhr claims that historically this "dualist" position arises as a response to the Synthesizing model. According to the dualists, the fundamental issue for Christians is not the challenge between church and culture or between nature and culture. Rather it is between human righteousness and God's righteousness. God comes to us in wrath against sin, in ourselves and in culture, but comes to us in mercy in Christ. Thus the paradox; both of these must be recognized as true. Human beings are radically fallen. The institutions of culture hold back corruption as much as possible, awaiting God's inbreaking to make the ultimate necessary changes. Niebuhr finds this teaching in the Bible most significantly in Paul's writings, and interprets Paul to be concerned only about inward change in people. One should not expect much from either culture or from the Christian community as a whole.

Billy Graham fits in this camp, and this approach appears largely assumed by those who are identified with the pietist and revivalist movements. Perhaps the closest group to this model found in the Bible is the Pharisees at the time of Jesus. This is not because of hypocrisy, with which they are often associated. Rather it is because they put tremendous emphasis upon the individual person's relationship with God and following God's will and instructions. Yet they had relatively little interest in the structures of society around them, either to affirm them or to challenge them.

A problem with this approach is that, as Jim Wallis puts it, our relationship with God is "personal, but never private."[89] Those who adopt this approach have a strong sense of personal right and wrong but do not think in terms of challenging injustice on a large scale or trying to make structures of society serve all people more equitably. Faith of this sort is socially irrelevant, never allowed to engage the larger world. Jesus is not allowed to be Lord of all; seemingly one changes uniforms when stepping into distinct arenas.

A common illustration is that a police officer may be required to use violent force against burglars as part of his job, but when he returns home and removes his badge, he must love his enemy and turn the other check if his own home is burglarized. In contrast, however, early followers of Jesus were oppressed by government and other leaders precisely because they declared Jesus to be Lord in all areas of life, and obeyed his instructions while rejecting those of other leaders.

4. Transforming. This model emphasizes *transforming* the structures of society and typically involves using power in godly ways. Those who take this approach ("Christ the Transformer of Culture") believe power can be used wisely and lovingly for the benefit of all, and advocate the selective and just use of violence when seen to be necessary. Note that the term *transforming* does not refer to personal transformation, though such Christians as well as many others believe that God wants us all to grow to be more like Christ.

This approach traces its roots to the "Reformed" branch of the Christian family, begun by Ulrich Zwingli and John Calvin. Like Luther, these two rejected the two-level distortion of vocation, believing that God calls people to areas of service beyond so-called "sacred" or "full-time" ministry. They also opened themselves to the equal-level distortion. Calvin believed that God called people to a variety of professions. The appropriateness of the profession could be tested by its ability to support the broader social community. Thus, certain possibilities were excluded, such as keeping a brothel or becoming a criminal. This is the approach Niebuhr discusses last, apparently his favorite because he can find no weaknesses in it worth mentioning.[90] Others, however, have noted some possible shortcomings for this model.

The insight of this category is that God is Lord of the universe, and God is in the process of making all things new (Isa. 48:3; 2 Cor. 5:17; Rev. 21:5). Jesus' parable of the mustard seed suggests that God works from small things, often slowly, to accomplish great things (Matt. 13:31-32). Niebuhr notes that this approach, like the previous, emphasizes Jesus as Redeemer more than teacher and model. There is a more hopeful approach to culture here than in the Confessing and Secluding approaches (discussed next). This is not a rejection of human beings as radically fallen, but there is hope that God can and will change things gradually. Niebuhr argues that this is present most deeply in the gospel of John, based largely on the affirmation of creation represented by Jesus' incarnation. However, most scholars find in John a rejection of culture in favor of God's community (more like the Confessing position).

Niebuhr finds Augustine to be a great illustration of this approach, for his conversion from paganism to Christianity coincided with the change of the Roman Empire to embracing a Christian worldview. Other examples include Columbus, Cromwell, and the Christian socialism of F. D. Maurice.

Two difficulties of this approach are (1) that it finds ethical leadership in Jesus' life and teachings, yet is willing to compromise these elements for pragmatic reasons, and (2) that in its attempt (often gently) to move institutions of culture in the direction of justice, it can end up supporting the injustices of those very structures. In the Bible, the situation closest to that advocated by the Transforming position may be Old Testament Israel during the period of the monarchy. This was an up and down time of political leadership and managing the gift of land; yet the biblical narrator gives high praise to kings such as David, Hezekiah, and Josiah despite their shortcomings. Some historical evidence indicates that Israel during the exile in Babylonia participated in local government.

5. Confessing. We come now to Niebuhr's fifth category of five, which he addresses first in his book. He called this "Christ against Culture," the most radical of the approaches, and the one with which he has the least patience. He describes this approach as "the one that uncompromisingly affirms the sole authority of Christ over the Christian and resolutely rejects culture's claims to loyalty."[91] That is, Jesus, by his life and teachings, is the model to follow (1 Pet. 2:21-23). Niebuhr articulates well the insight of this approach that Christians are to follow the principle of Christ's Lordship; this seems to be the approach taken by the earliest Christians. He indeed finds this attitude within the New Testament, particularly in the books of 1 John and Revelation, as well as in "best-loved" early Christian writings, such as *The Teaching of the Twelve, The Shepherd of Hermas, The Epistle of Barnabas,* and the *First Epistle of Clement.* In fact, it is the category that comes closest to the practice of Jesus himself in Niebuhr's understanding.

Because Niebuhr failed to distinguish two versions among those who take this approach, a separate category has been added (called "Secluding," see below). What both this and the next have in common, and what subjects them to Niebuhr's ire, is that they particularly refuse to embrace, even in principle, the possibility of employing power structures to accomplish the instructions of Christ.

Additional historical examples of this approach include Tertullian (ca. 160–220) and the sixteenth-century Anabaptists, e.g., Menno Simons. More recent examples include Dietrich Bonhoeffer, whose work with the so-called "Confessing" church of Germany during the Nazi era suggested the label for this approach. Bonhoeffer insisted that in regard to unjust practices of government, the church must not cooperate but must *confess* Jesus Christ as Lord. Martin Luther King Jr. also fits here, who challenged unjust laws and structures in U.S. society (pursuing the *goals* of Jesus) but insisted on operating nonviolently (operating by the *way* of Jesus). Also we can note William Penn and Desmond Tutu. A possible biblical example of the Confessing approach is Israel in exile, where they are instructed to seek the good of the city in which they find themselves, yet are ultimately loyal to a kingdom from elsewhere, that is, God's kingdom (Jer. 29:1-14). It would appear that the early church, as reflected in the book of Acts, likewise showed respect to those in authority positions, yet took their instructions from the teachings of Jesus and the direction of the Holy Spirit (e.g., Acts 4:18-20).

People who adopt this model work toward the transformation of society and its structures, but they are also concerned to follow Jesus' *way* of doing things. For this reason, they refuse to employ violent power even when it appears that this is the most effective short-term way of responding to evil actions. They are less confident in the potential goodness of structures, but more confident in the ability of people to follow Christ and his ways by God's grace. They establish alternative options.

Niebuhr acknowledges, with a touch of irony, the contributions of such Christians: "intending to abolish all methods of coercion, [they] have helped to reform prisons, to limit armaments, and to establish international organizations for the maintenance of peace through coercion."[92] Such groups provide valuable warnings lest the church become coopted and manipulated as an arm of the government. However, he finds the approach inadequate. First, it is inconsistent: even such radical groups inevitably make use of the benefits of the state. So they fool themselves into thinking they are separate when they really are not. Another problem is that sin is assumed to be in the culture and purity within the believing community, which fails to adequately account for sin in the community itself. Further, such groups tend to be rigid and practice a denial of grace. Finally, Niebuhr is concerned that such groups practice a denial of the goodness of creation and God's plan to rule over it through human beings. Another way of phrasing the latter concern is that the group's focus on faithfulness could cause shortcomings in accomplishing the goals of Jesus and God's kingdom, goals such as justice and compassion for all.

6. Secluding. This category (also "Christ against Culture," see discussion above) is for those who address their commitment to Christ by seeking a separate geographical location within which to live out their obedience. Like the Confessing approach, this one advocates Jesus' life and teachings as a model to follow. The assumption of such groups is that they cannot follow Christ faithfully while at the same time participating deeply in a society organized around other values or some other lord.

Groups who live by this model form separate communities with their own schools and other institutions. Such include the Benedictines, Antony of Egypt (and other monastic movements), the Amish, early Quakers, Leo Tolstoy, and Dutch society in which Protestants and Catholics had their own separate locations and institutions. All of these in different ways sought to create a society structured on the teachings of Jesus that would serve as a model "city on a hill" (Matt. 5:14), a beacon light of hope and truth that would draw others to join their community. Possible biblical examples include Israel, during its sojourn in Egypt, living as a secluded community in the land of Goshen, and the Essenes before and during the time of Jesus, Jews who lived in the wilderness and performed their own religious services.[93]

The insight of this approach is that the Bible envisions Christians in a genuine physical and human community in which they demonstrate they are Christ's disciples by the love they show for each other (John 13:34-35). Its dangers are the same as those in the Confessing category, heightened by the increased difficulty of engaging with those outside of the community due to physical and social boundaries.

Confessing and Transforming

In the descriptions above, it was my intent to show on the one hand the insight of each approach, and thus what we have to learn from those who adopt it. On the other hand, I also sought to show the limitation or difficulty associated with each, and thus again why those who adopt one position need to hear from those who, in an effort to be faithful, take another.

Much, though not all, of the Evangelical Christian world finds itself today in the Transforming camp. Historically, those from an Anabaptist heritage are among those who adopt the Confessing approach (and some in the Secluding). As an illustration of how such groups can learn from each other, here is a brief description of similarities and differences, and thus opportunities for conversation. The Transforming position is the more pragmatic, seeking to act in ways that produce visible change. The Confessing position is more concerned to be faithful to the instructions and model life of Jesus, and to trust God to work through such efforts even if it means not being so directly pragmatic.

Transforming and Confessing IN COMMON

- Christian faith is different and has something to offer
- Church must remain distinct from culture
- Christian faith is not private and should not be reclusive
- Christian faith should engage culture
- Jesus' life and teachings should be taken seriously

DIFFERENCES

Transforming	Confessing
• Begins from the Creation Mandate	• Begins with a vision of a new creation
• Makes the old better, serves by transforming institutions	• Rejects the old, serves by starting something new
• Takes what Scripture says about the church and Israel and applies it analogously to the world (complementary roles, gifts)	• No dependable trust in people
	• Parable of weeds in the field means wait to remove evildoers
• The call to be salt and light means helping change institutions	• Parable of sheep and goats means faithful effort more important than results
• Emphasizes all for the glory of God	• Acts, early church: faithful not effective
• Parable of the talents means pragmatic action	• Not as serving people but serving the Lord
• Parable of the mustard seed = visible change	• Parable of the mustard seed = invisible change
• Risk: Violating the *way* of Jesus and his mission	• Risk: Failing to accomplish the *goals* of Jesus' mission

The Heart of the Six Options

For those who are committed to a worldview other than what is found in the Bible, the six categories described above may need to be adapted and some of their assumptions replaced. However, in most cases each of the six models should provide a possible option for the way those who adopt your worldview can relate to the culture around them. Here is an attempt to define the "heart" or central principles of each option.

Capitulating. This category fits those of whatever worldview who are also Pluralists or who otherwise emphasize that human beings need to work together to find common values and goals. You believe in your worldview, but you don't wish to impose it on someone else, partly because you think that other worldviews work just fine for other people.

Synthesizing. This fits those who are pragmatic about getting things done, believe that no one worldview offers all that is needed, and believe that power can be used benevolently to accomplish good goals. It is less cooperative and more demanding than the Capitulating approach.

Privatizing. This is for those who emphasize that religious and worldview matters are of only private concern, and are confident that good ethical decisions can be made within the organizations (including government) that address policies and values for each profession and institution separately.

Transforming. This fits those who are convinced of the rightness of their worldview and have the confidence to join with people, both of the same worldview and not, to make positive changes in society and its institutions. It embraces persuasion and has hope for gradual change but is also willing to use force and violence to some extent in pursuit of goals.

Confessing. This position is also for those convinced of the rightness of their worldview and who hope for gradual positive change in society. This group also embraces persuasion, but will only use nonviolent methods to promote change. Such people would rather suffer harm than inflict it on others. They tend to establish alternative structures rather than change existing ones.

Secluding. For those who are convinced that people who hold to a particular worldview should work together to establish their own institutions and neighborhoods. They seek to obtain land rights in specific geographical areas and attempt to live together in ways they hope others will recognize, affirm, and join.

Revisiting Your Mission Statement

In chapter 3 we discussed the possibility of a mission statement in the context of personal reflection upon various clues and indicators, such as one's passions, history, and giftedness (SHAPE). The present discussion as well as chapters 6 and 10 have been an invitation to think about the corporate dimension of calling. One's mission statement should take this broader dimension into account as well. What will it mean to partner with others to accomplish the tasks of your calling? How will you relate to your culture in a group, such as the church or something else? How will your work in a business or organization be affected by those beliefs you have in common and those that differ from those around you? For example, will you challenge unethical practices? Will you use your influence to change policies?

The Message of Reconciliation

Two accounts illustrate how the actions of a small group can have a significant impact on troubling issues in their society. The first is from South Africa. After decades of apartheid and centuries of conflict between persons of African and European descent, a transition of power took place between F. W. de Klerk and Nelson Mandela. Leaders from multiple social groups considered how the country might best move forward after generations of oppression, abuse, and brutality. Out of these deliberations came a council named the Truth and Reconciliation Commission. Persons who were wronged or whose family members were hurt or killed could bring their grievances before this body. The process also allowed for amnesty for those who would confess their crimes and seek reconciliation.

In one case, a man admitted to the brutal torture and killing of a young man. The victim's mother offered to accept the appeal for amnesty on behalf of her son, but asked for two things. First, she wanted to see where her child had been burned to death so that she might recover some ashes for a memorial. Second, she requested that the murderer be required to spend time in her home on a regular basis because she needed someone to love now, and this man needed love. The Commission has provided a way to bring closure to the call for vengeance without ignoring or trivializing the terrible injustices that were committed.

The second account comes from Israel and Palestine. In the midst of ongoing tensions and difficulties over land, groups on opposite sides of the conflict have begun to come together for mutual grieving and consultation. One such group is known as Combatants for Peace, composed of former Israeli soldiers and Palestinian freedom fighters. These people have amazingly learned to trust one another enough to listen to each other's stories and to deliberate together on nonviolent ways to make improvement on issues that involve their society. When asked what motivated them to take such risks to meet with one another, one man responded, "I knew there had to be a better way. The acts of violence being used on both sides were not helping to make any progress." The actions of a small group have power to address questions that affect an entire culture.

Questions for Reflection and Discussion
1.   Which of the six Christ and Culture categories is closest to reflecting what the Bible teaches? Why do you believe so?
2.   Which of the six models is closest to your own way of engaging culture? Do you think this is the best way? Or are you open to change?
3.   How does your model align with the life and teachings of Jesus? How important is it to follow Jesus' own way of relating to culture?

4. Chapter 6 concludes with two stories, one in Le Chambon, France, and the other in Timisoara, Romania. Reflect on the values and assumptions that may lie behind the actions taken by Christians in each context. Which of the "Christ and Culture" categories seem to be employed in each situation? Explain why you think so.
5. What issues in your culture should be engaged? Why?
6. Review the chart at the beginning of this chapter. Do the worldview categories there—McWorld, Jihad, Mustard Seed—align with any of the six Christ and Culture categories? If so, how?
7. What tensions and problems are current in your culture? What ideas do you have for helping to make positive changes?

Suggestions for Further Reading

D. A. Carson, *Christ and Culture Revisited*. Grand Rapids, MI: Eerdmans, 2008.

Craig A. Carter, *Rethinking* Christ and Culture: *A Post-Christendom Perspective*. Grand Rapids, MI: Brazos, 2006.

Duane K. Friesen, *Artists, Citizens, Philosophers: Seeking the Peace of the City*. Scottdale, PA: Herald, 2000.

Glen H. Stassen, D. M. Yeager, and John Howard Yoder, *Authentic Transformation: A New Vision of Christ and Culture*. Nashville, TN: Abingdon, 1996.

Tom Sine, *The Mustard Seed Conspiracy*. Waco, TX: Word, 1981.

_____, *Mustard Seed versus McWorld: Reinventing Life and Faith for the Future*. Grand Rapids, MI: Baker, 1999.

Part 3

Going Forth:
Work and Vocation

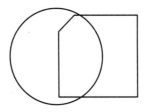

CHAPTER 12
The Bible and Work

In this final section of the book, we examine a Christian understanding of work and vocation. The present chapter summarizes the legacy of Western understandings of work and places that in contrast to what the Bible says on the subject.

Western Approaches to Work

The tension between order and freedom on display in the film *Pleasantville* is one significant legacy of approaches to culture and society in the West. Attitudes toward work have also been passed down through the generations. For some thinkers and cultures, work was viewed as a curse. We find this, for example, among certain ancient Greeks, such as Plato and Aristotle. They taught that the ideal was for the elite in society to think about the good and the beautiful while others did the essential manual labor of the town or community. In fact, the word *school* derives from the Greek term *schole*, originally meaning "leisure."

Something similar played out in the Medieval period during which the active work of ordinary Christian citizens was not valued as highly as the contemplative life of the monk (though monks also did manual labor). In the twentieth century, Sigmund Freud argued that work is an inescapable and tragic necessity, a form of self-denial. The ideal, he said, was to live a life of leisure, but because humans are insecure, they trade pleasure for security. So that is one major strand of Western legacy: work is a curse to be avoided if possible.[94]

A slightly more hopeful approach was offered during the Renaissance, the great celebration of all things beautiful and artistic. Most work is unworthy of human beings, the reasoning went, but creativity made one like God. Thus the artist became the ideal, and artistic expression was considered noble. Centuries later, Karl Marx picked up the idea of the nobility of work but broadened it to include more than just artistry. He taught that work for most persons is degrading; but, he promised, a revolution was coming that would set the oppressed free and enable all persons to find their proper role in society, a role in which they would perform based on their true gifts and abilities. So both the Renaissance celebration of the artist and Karl Marx's revolutionary vision are a second aspect of work's legacy in the West: work under the right conditions has potential to bring self-fulfillment.

We can see this double legacy among members of Western cultures today. For many, work is a curse. At best, it is a way to keep alive, but mostly it is something to be avoided. For others, work is a source of self-fulfillment. It is a way of being rewarded for one's gifts and abilities. One version of the latter is empire building. Work is a way of controlling others for the sake of one's own advancement and accomplishment. A further complication is the tendency toward individualism in European and North American cultures. As a result, whatever community-enhancing elements there have been in these two approaches to work have become severely limited. Work has become an activity for accomplishing one's own goals and only secondarily for the benefit of others.

This mixed legacy plays out in the tension we saw between order and freedom in our discussion of *Pleasantville* (ch. 10). It has also distilled into two of the four primary motivations among those in the work force, described in chapter 2: *Live for the Weekend* (self-centered and pessimistic about work), and *My Empire* (self-centered and optimistic about work). As you may have realized, the last approach of the four (*Service*, which is *others*-centered and optimistic about work) is closest to vocation, the secondary calling, that is the focus of this book. Among other things, vocation means to care about service, trusting that one's own needs will be met.

The Bible and Work

In chapter 5, we reviewed a summary of the concepts and values of a Christian worldview as found in the Bible. In particular, we noted the four themes known as "God's Design." God is at work in the world and invites us to participate in that work. We now take a closer look at the Bible's approach to work. If the Bible's vision of *shalom* is rooted in the nature of God, what does that have to do with the place of human beings in the world? The remainder of this chapter explores the Bible's basis for human purpose and mission.

God Works. It is helpful to recognize that God models work. We see this at the very beginning of the Bible, which describes how God labors for six days and then rests on the seventh (Gen. 1:1–2:4). A brief overview of the remainder of the Bible illustrates how God, contrary to what some may have thought, has not been resting ever since. Quite the contrary! God does not sleep (Ps. 121:4).

In the book of Genesis, we find God monitoring the creation and intervening with corrective action. We see this notably in three acts: sending the flood to destroy a rebellious creation (Gen. 6), confusing language and dispersing the nations when people undertook an unhealthy project (Gen. 11), and establishing a special people through the calling of Abraham and Sarah (Gen. 12). From this point, the narrative focuses particularly on this family, its struggles, and its deliverance to the land of promise. However, there are repeated indicators that God also has great interest in other peoples, their actions, and their needs.

God continually calls human beings to share in the work. In fact, it is rare to find an activity of God in which humans do not play a role. God even consults particular persons before making certain decisions. With the coming of Jesus, God is intimately involved in sending messengers with announcements, directing and providing for Jesus and his disciples, and delivering some of the disciples from dire circumstances. One of the most notable declarations of God's work comes when Jesus was accused of healing a man on the Sabbath, a day God had set aside for rest. "My Father is still working," said Jesus, "and I also am working" (John 5:17 NRSV). Not only was God working but was working to heal a man on the Sabbath!

In summary, we can see both that God is an active, working being, and that God wants human beings involved with this work. How does the Bible present this picture?

The Creation Mandate. It all starts back at the beginning of the Bible. In the first chapter of Genesis, God creates human beings, male and female, in the divine image and gives them a specific responsibility: to *rule over* the rest of creation (Gen. 1:26-28). The original Hebrew words are very clear in their royal connotation, a theme that continues through the Bible (cf. Luke 22:30; 2 Tim. 2:12), even to the book of Revelation (see Rev. 20:4, 6; 22:5). According to Genesis 1, human beings have the status of royalty in their relationship with the rest of the creation and are accountable for it.

In the very next chapter, we find a different though complementary image. Human beings are placed in a garden and given instructions: "to work it and take care of it" (Gen. 2:15). The Hebrew verbs here could be translated *serve* and *guard*. The idea is that human beings have a servant role, to provide for and protect the garden. This role complements the royal image: humans must never become arrogant toward the rest of God's creation. They relate to it both as master and as servant.

Loss of Paradise. Human disobedience complicated the process by which all must accomplish their basic needs (pain in childbirth, thistles, sweat; Gen. 3:16-19). Human collaboration may be dangerous in its rebellion against God (Gen. 11:1-9). Yet work has dignity and can still be joyful, though it is more difficult than God's original design during this period of anticipation for God to restore creation (Isa. 2:4; 65:22-23).

One of the central themes in Ecclesiastes is toil, which the author says is vapor (often translated *vanity*) and a futile effort. He addresses all four of the typical ways people in our society approach work. He knows the oppression of those who struggle to keep alive (4:1-3). He points out some of the distortions of work: the futility of living for the weekends (pleasure, 2:1-3); the emptiness of empire building (2:4-11), work addiction, and effort motivated by envy (4:4-8)—interestingly traps similar to those that hinder the growth of the seed in Jesus' parable of the soils (Mark 4:3-20). He urges his readers to simplicity, contentment, and cooperative efforts in community (Eccl. 4:9-12). In addition, he highlights the biblical theme of accountability (see 5:8–6:9).

Ecclesiastes also directs its readers to the possibility of satisfaction in their efforts and encourages work with enthusiasm (3:13; 5:18; 9:1-10). In a world of uncertainty, the author urges both diligence and generosity (10:16–11:6), anticipating Jesus' instruction to "give, and it will be given to you" (Luke 6:38). That is, he recognizes that God wants humans to find satisfaction in their work as a gift from God; paradoxically, this cannot be earned but only received gratefully. Work should be done, not only to accomplish one's own needs, but to share with others (cf. Deut. 15:10; Eph. 4:28).[95]

The Example and Teaching of Jesus. Jesus, in his mission to bring God's salvation, modeled a rhythm of work and rest (Mark 6:31), promised rest (Matt. 11:28-29), and taught his disciples to trust that God would care for their needs more than for the birds and flowers (Matt. 6:25-34). He taught that the Sabbath was given to human beings as a gift (Mark 2:27). The New Testament writers affirm the dignity of work, to care for one's family, to share with those in need (Eph. 4:28; 2 Thess. 3:10-13; 1 Tim. 5:8), and to anticipate the new creation (Rom. 8:19-22; Rev. 21:1–22:5).

The Great Commission. A second major assignment is given to human beings and, like the Creation Mandate, it has two parts. Jesus instructed his disciples, on the basis of the authority given him, to "Therefore go and make disciples of all nations, baptizing them in the name of the Father and of the Son and of the Holy Spirit, and teaching them to obey everything I have commanded you" (Matt. 28:19-20). He concludes by encouraging them that his presence will remain with them all the way to the end of the age. The first part of this commission is to invite people to faith, represented by baptism, which initiates them by public confession into the people of God. The second part is to nurture that faith through teaching. Both parts are necessary in order to "make disciples." As the Apostle Paul explains, this is a ministry of reconciliation (2 Cor. 5:18), first being reconciled to God (Rom. 5:10) and then also reconciled with human beings (Eph. 2:11-22).

Vocation: God's Calling

We can now ask the questions toward which we have been moving. Does the above information mean that all Christians should be pastors or church planters or missionaries or worship leaders? Does God today call anyone to be scientists, public school teachers, businesspeople, and coaches?

To answer these questions, we need to review what we find in the Bible. We noted above that God's creation of humans begins with the two-part Creation Mandate: to rule over and to serve the creation. If we search, we will find that the Bible never tells us stories or gives us instructions about God calling people to be carpenters, or school teachers, or shepherds, or brick layers. On the other hand, we actually see people *leaving* professions because of God's call, such as some of Jesus' disciples who left fishing and tax collecting. These two facts may lead us to suspect that God is *really* calling all people to religious leadership, if they would only pay attention.

Yet if we think about it a bit further, could everyone be in those kinds of roles? What would that look like? If we examine the Bible carefully, we see three things in this regard:

- First, the Bible talks about God giving people aptitudes in a variety of areas, for example, artistic gifts for the beautiful furnishings of the tabernacle (e.g., Exod. 28:3; 31:1-11; 35:35; 36:1) and trade skills for constructing the temple (1 Kings 7:14). It is also interesting to ponder how much the aptitudes and the skills developed in one profession might be beneficial for a person who later switched to another. For example, Moses spent years as a shepherd of sheep before he received his dramatic call from God to shepherd the people of Israel.

- Second, there seems to be no occasion in the Bible when a profession is rejected *as* a profession, with two probable exceptions: sorcery and prostitution, considered to be immoral (Deut. 18:10-11; 23:17). We don't find accounts celebrating certain professions and criticizing others. Instead, we find all people challenged in a variety of ways, for example, to be just and honorable people. In some professions, however, it may be difficult to follow Jesus' instructions whole heartedly.[96]
- Third, not all people who respond to the call of Jesus or of the apostles actually leave their profession. Paul continued his craft of tentmaking, a profession also followed by Priscilla and Aquila (Acts 18:1-3). We also have no indication that Zaccheus left his job as a tax collector; instead, he became a more honest and just collector of taxes. The key issue: what they did now fit into a bigger plan called God's kingdom.
- Finally, we should notice that the Apostle Paul begins his counsel about work by assuming that Christians can serve God within the employment where they find themselves. In 1 Corinthians 7:20-24, Paul encourages believers to be content in their jobs.[97]

So, to summarize, even though the Bible has no accounts of God *directly* calling someone to tasks such as farming, business, school teaching, and other professional matters, the *indirect* indication is that God does indeed equip people for such places where their gifts can be used to help others.

Distortions of Calling

Chapter 3 described three callings: the primary (everyone's call to relationship with God and God's people), the secondary = vocation (each person's call to a specific mission), and the immediate (our daily tasks). The approach to the secondary calling (vocation) argued in the previous section was succinctly expressed by my student Cory Frey when he said, "Not all of us are called to make our profession as a minister. But all of us are called to be ministers in our profession."

This approach stands in contrast with two other approaches that are frequently labeled *distortions* of calling; these have plagued Christians throughout the past millennia. The first is the *Two-Level Distortion* of vocation. This is the understanding that there are two levels of obedience and faith to God: the ideal level and the permitted level (sometimes distinguished as a sacred profession vs. a secular one or the contemplative life vs. the active life). According to this distortion, God really wants everyone to choose the ideal life, by becoming a pastor or other leader, but will tolerate those who are not quite that dedicated or adventurous.

A positive inclination in this approach is that we should indeed aim for what God asks of us even if it may seem daunting. However, one of the problems with this distortion is that it might motivate someone to pursue a certain religious leadership role when that was never God's call for them. Another is that a person might correctly choose a so-called "secular" profession and then forever feel shame for not having enough faith to take a religious leadership role.

A second mistake is the *Equal-Level Distortion* of vocation. This is the understanding that all work is on an equal level for God's purposes, that anything we choose to do is as acceptable to God as anything else. This perspective gets it right that God calls people to a broad variety of roles in life. However, this distortion can lead someone to "settle" for something less than God's true call on the grounds that all work is equal. It can, in addition, lead to work addiction, for it would seem that the more productive one is the more likely to be pleasing to God. This distortion, with its interest in productivity may make one a bit more prone to the problem of empire building, or holding the secondary calling in a place of higher importance than God. We will return to the latter issue.

Love, God's Design, and Vocation

The chart below depicts the relationship among the primary and secondary callings and the four biblical themes of God's Design (SCAR) presented in chapter 5. It also represents how the two great assignments (CM and GC) are infused with the two great commandments: loving God and loving neighbor; love *motivates* our work so that it aligns with God's goals and contributes to what is best for others. Love of God is the root and ground of everything else, and love of neighbor overflows from the believing community to everywhere else. You cannot love God without also loving your neighbor, and you cannot love your neighbor without also loving God (1 John 3:16-18; James 2). The vertical line down the center of the "Primary and Secondary Callings" column is to remind us that for each of these elements there are both individual and corporate dimensions (explained below).

God's Design (SCAR)		Primary and Secondary Callings	
Loving Neighbor	Abundant Life	Secondary Calling:	Creation Mandate
	Salvation	Secondary Calling:	Great Commission
	Community	Primary Calling:	God's People (Church)
	Relationship w/God	Primary Calling:	Worship
		Loving God	

- *Abundant Life:* The Creation Mandate involves establishing the context and opportunity for abundant life, all that humans need to live and thrive. The secondary calling of some persons is mostly in this area. They may have a very specific job, e.g., farming, that provides food for others. They likely will also participate to some extent with a group, e.g., a grain elevator company where they work with others toward these goals.
- *Salvation*: The Great Commission involves inviting persons to faith and nurturing them to be disciples of Jesus Christ. The secondary calling of some persons is mostly in this area. They may be a cross-cultural missionary, a priest, or another church leader. They could also work with a group to do evangelistic and discipleship work in their community.
- *Community*: God calls everyone to be part of a covenanting and worshiping community. Each person has gifts given by the Holy Spirit for service in their particular body

of Christ. The whole body also functions to achieve goals of love and service for others.

- *Relationship with God*: God calls everyone into a love relationship with their Creator. Human beings worship God both in deliberate times and places set aside for that purpose, and in an ongoing way in all aspects of life. An individual relationship with God is cultivated through spiritual disciplines, such as prayer, Bible reading, fasting, and meditation. Humans also need to love and worship God corporately, one of the most important aspects of being a community together.

In short, God's call on our lives involves all four of these: God calls us to loving *relationships* with our Creator and with *others* that involve promoting *salvation* and *abundant life*.

Questions for Reflection and Discussion
1. How would you summarize what the Bible says about work?
2. What indications of the Western legacy regarding work do you notice around you? How do these connect with the four attitudes toward work, Staying Alive, Live for the Weekend, My Empire, and Service?
3. Which of the two major distortions of vocation—the Two-Level and the Equal-Level—is more of a temptation for you? Why do you think this is the case?
4. Are you convinced that the two distortions described here are actual problems? Even if ultimately they are errors, what partial truth does each contain?

Suggestions for Further Reading
Douglas J. Schuurman, *Vocation: Discerning Our Callings in Life.* Grand Rapids, MI: Eerdmans, 2004.
Gordon T. Smith, *Courage and Calling*, 2nd ed. Downers Grove, IL: InterVarsity, 2011.

CHAPTER 13

Your Job and Your Vocation

Warren Schmidt is about to retire, leaving the world of work behind. And he finds it quite unsettling. In the film *About Schmidt* (directed and cowritten by Alexander Payne), we watch the clock's second hand tick along until it is exactly 5:00 p.m.[98] Warren (played by Jack Nicholson) has been an actuary in Omaha, Nebraska, and his office is surrounded with boxes. Later we see that these boxes have been moved to company storage where they will be used no more. There is a nice retirement party at a local restaurant. People say nice things, really nice things. Warren has done a good job. People appreciate that. But we sense that Warren is beginning to wonder what it was all about. Has he lived his life for the things that really matter? Family, friends, work colleagues? A job that contributed to the good of people's lives? He wants to share his wisdom with the new upstart who took his position, but Warren is not needed.

His wife, Helen (June Squibb), surprises him with breakfast in their new thirty-five foot Winnebago Adventurer. But Warren anticipates no adventure. His life had no purpose before, and he can't imagine finding one now. He has lived his life in a blur. Even the special friendship he thought was genuine gets cast in a more troubling light.

Then there is a twist in the story line. Warren and Helen's daughter, Jeannie (Hope Davis), is about to be married in Denver to Randall Hertzel (Dermot Mulroney), a simpleton of a waterbed salesman whom Warren despises. In the final months before the wedding, Helen suddenly dies, leaving Warren to think about the ways he has failed both wife and daughter. On a journey in his Winnebago, he has something of an epiphany and decides his calling is to make sure the marriage never happens. But in this too he fails, and he must journey miserably back to his big empty house.

One ray of hope glows in this story, however. Earlier, Warren stumbled across a TV ad and has been sending monthly checks to support a six-year-old orphan in Tanzania. This boy has become a confessor figure to Warren, who sends letters describing the frustrations and disappointments he is encountering. When Warren returns home and starts through his accumulated mail, he finds a letter from a woman caretaker for little Ndugu. Tears fill Warren's eyes as he realizes that this boy has benefited from his gifts, has appreciated his letters, and now has included a simple crayon drawing as an expression of gratitude.

Definition of Work

The story of Warren Schmidt is a cautionary tale for those who would define their lives only in terms of a stable job, a good paycheck, and a comfortable material lifestyle. As we consider some of the more specific details about the work world, we need to be clear about what we mean by *work*. The term *work* can be defined in a variety of ways depending on its context. Most basically it has to do with "activity in which one exerts strength or faculties to do or perform something."[99] A scientific definition is "force acting on an object to cause displacement." Sometimes we use the term subjectively to indicate any effort we find to be drudgery.

An excellent definition for the way in which we will use *work* in our discussion of vocation is provided by theologian Miroslav Volf:

> Work is honest, purposeful, and methodologically specified social activity whose primary goal is the creation of products or states of affairs that can satisfy the needs of working individuals or their cocreatures, or (if primarily an end in itself) activity that is necessary in order for acting individuals to satisfy their needs apart from the need for the activity itself.[100]

More concisely, *work is honest, purposeful, mutually beneficial social activity exerted in order to meet the needs of people either directly or indirectly, whether compensated or not.*

- Work is honest and purposeful (this eliminates crime and randomness, and addresses purpose);
- Work is mutually beneficial social activity that meets needs (this eliminates destruction, slavery, and subjectivity); and
- Work may address goals directly or indirectly, whether or not compensated (addresses preparation, such as education, and allows for that which is voluntary).

This general definition acknowledges our human lot, that we must somehow provide for our needs and for those of others under our care. It is the assumption here that God calls people to work, except in unusual circumstances such as disability.[101] Work is a significant way in which the needs of people are met, the way we love and serve one another.

Job and Vocation

In view of the understanding of work presented above, and the concept of vocation presented in previous chapters, we turn now to various possible relationships between two areas of work: a vocation and a job (or profession). *Vocation* is the arena of work that involves one's deep sense of call and purpose in life. *Job* is the arena of work that results in earning money.

(Two theoretical options will *not* be described below. The first is a job without a vocation, the plight of Warren Schmidt. This, I propose, is never a reality for a Christian person—though one could be unaware of one's vocation—nor would it be a satisfying existence for anyone else. Second, there might be a situation in which the job and the vocation achieve a precise overlap. While this may occasionally happen, I believe what seem like "perfect jobs" most often fit the first model below.)

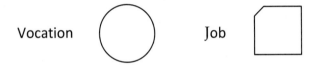

Vocation   Job

1. *Job fits within the Vocation.* Sometimes, to do the job is to do the vocation. Yet there are aspects of the vocation that may not fit the job. An example could be a counselor who works for a Christian or other psychology practice where the policies and values align completely with those of the employee in question. Yet she or he may also counsel outside the job, with or without pay.

2. *Vocation fits within the Job.* To do the vocation is to do the job. Yet there are aspects of the job that do not fit the vocation. A possible example could be the pastor of a church who does not feel gifted to do administrative parts of the job description though very strong in other roles, such as preaching and relating to those who are part of the church.

3. *Vocation is separate from a Job.* In this case, there is no job that brings in money. Rather, support comes from elsewhere. Common examples include missionaries or those who participate in various outreach and service organizations without pay. Parents and retired persons who volunteer to work at a food bank would also fit this option.[102]

4. *Vocation is alongside a Job.* For some people, their job has little to do with their vocation (though it should still be done as an act of service.) For example, a carpenter whose ministry is leading boys clubs on the weekend and a businesswoman who leads mission trips several times per year may fit this option.

5. *Vocation overlaps with a Job.* Our final job/vocation relationship means that parts of the job do and other parts do not fit the vocation. Likewise, parts of the vocation are and parts are not accomplished by the job. One example could be a nurse whose job is in some ways like option 2: some parts of the job don't fit her vocation. Yet, like option 1, she also volunteers in a clinic for low-income people in addition to her regular job. Similarly, a computer programmer might be in a job in which some aspects don't fit his vocation, and who does work outside the job, such as traveling annually to Haiti for a few weeks to voluntarily assist small business people with their computer equipment.[103]

These five options are to some extent caricatures, and yet it can be helpful to consider which of these is most like the situation you are in currently or anticipate in the future. The better you can be clear on what parts of your life are vocation, the better you can keep your job or profession in proper perspective, especially when situations arise that may cause you to think about a change of location, job, or profession.

Dualities of Your Vocation
Suppose you have taken up some of the suggestions found in chapter 3 for understanding yourself. You have examined the traps often lurking in our society and have begun to cultivate the more healthy identity statements found in the Bible. You have reflected on the elements found in the SHAPE acronym, and are starting to see some possibilities for following the dots to what might be a vocation that suits you well. You have considered the Job and Vocation options described above, and see that one of them might apply to where you are headed.

Perhaps you have even written a personal mission statement and you feel ready for the next step in making this happen. What are some of the features you can expect in your particular adventure just ahead?

Here are a few that you can anticipate, if you have not encountered them already, listed in the form of dualities. The idea is that you will experience both elements in each case, though this will play out differently for each person.

Creation Mandate and Great Commission. As mentioned previously, since these are the two great assignments that God has given to human beings, each person needs to consider in what ways he or she contributes to both: (1) sustaining the world as well as (2) ways of sharing the Good News of faith in Christ and participating in his ministry of reconciling a broken world to God and to other persons. It may be especially challenging for those who are heavily invested in one to consider what aspects of the other may still be important. However, creative ways of witnessing to one's faith are practiced all the time, for example, by those in the insurance business, those who operate clothing stores, and those who serve in restaurants. The Great Commission might involve talking with a coworker or client about the issues of their life and sharing how your faith in Jesus has made a difference for you. It could include an ethical action that shocks others—taking a stand against injustice, or urging for adopting a company policy that reflects compassion—and leads them to ask why you did it. On the other hand, those who serve as missionaries, pastors, and evangelists have opportunities to participate in the Creation Mandate: to deliver food, repair stores and houses damaged by storms. and paint the rooms of neighbors and strangers.

Central and Peripheral. In the daily routines as well as the interruptions of life, you will find yourself doing some things that are very central to your vocation. These include matters both on the job/profession and beyond that, depending on the particular mix of job and vocation that is yours. This is where you want to put much of your creativity and energy, and where hopefully you will have a sense of satisfaction in doing well. Other things will be more peripheral. Certainly these will often include what Gordon Smith calls the "immediate call-ing," e.g., emergencies, helping a friend or a neighbor with something unexpected. But they also involve keeping the lawn mowed, shoveling snow off a sidewalk, making meals, clean-ing the house, and other mundane aspects of our existence.

General and Specific. The general aspects of your vocation are the broad field or discipline in which you are located. This could be music for professional musicians or business law for those in business. Other things are much more specific and specialized, such as the musical instrument played or the style of music mastered, the specific type of business and its very focused challenges. Most of our time is rightly spent on the specific, but we also need to remember and to learn from what is going on in the general dimension of our arena.

Corporate and Personal. Each of us will have a personal realm of responsibility and involvement, but with very few exceptions we will also participate in groups. The latter can include the company you work for, a community organization, and church structures of various kinds. The former includes your job assignment, such as plant foreman on the second shift, or chairperson of a committee. Challenges happen to us very much on both the corporate and the personal levels, but at any given time the need will likely be greater on one than the other.

Status and Journey. When we identify our secondary call-ing (vocation), it will likely involve a status, that is, something we can claim as part of our identity. Examples include a job title, a certification, and an educational achievement. Such in-dicators of status can be a source of satisfaction, though they also point to those things for which we are accountable: to be a good supervisor, to represent our educational institution well, and so on. Yet we are also on a journey, a process of growth in which we progress but never completely arrive in this life, a journey that may not always be smooth or predictable regard-less of the status implied by our job title.

Success and Failure. Part of the journey that was indicated in the previous paragraph involves success, the satisfaction that comes from accomplishing God's goals. Examples could include feeding hungry people, finishing a challenging assign-

ment, and getting a promotion. Even the most successful people also experience failure, whether involving personal character weaknesses, bad choices, or things out of our control.
Others' expectations of us may be unreasonable so that we may
succeed in God's eyes while failing in the eyes of others. We
may experience self-doubt, wondering if we are indeed in the
right job, profession, or vocation. Learning to deal emotionally
with both success and failure can be among the most challenging aspects of living out our vocation.

Clarity and Mystery. Life is full of both clarity and mystery. The former may include certainty about what Scripture
teaches as well as confidence that God has led us to a specific
job in a specific location. Examples include knowing that you
are called to love God first and foremost while loving your
neighbor comes a close second, knowing that being a servant to
those in your community is what gives a sense of purpose to
your day. Yet there will also be mystery, those things where
the Bible is silent or hard to understand, and times when direction is not so clear. Examples can include which church to join
and job choices of various kinds. We can rejoice in times of
clarity, but we also need to learn to trust God in times and
places of mystery. As the Apostle Paul said, "Now I know in
part; then I shall know fully, even as I am fully known" (1 Cor.
13:12b).

Vocation in the Anabaptist Tradition
Dualities such as those described above also play out within
Christian communities and organizations. Their history can be
instructive. Keith Graber Miller made an insightful study of
vocation in the Anabaptist tradition, that group of Christians
who originated in sixteenth-century Europe and whose descendants include Mennonite and Brethren groups today. These
Christians have almost exclusively embraced the Confessing
and Secluding models of culture engagement.[104]

Graber Miller points out how those in the Anabaptist family
have had a somewhat "tortured" history with the notion of
calling. For example, some crafts or professions were prohibit-
ed for such believers because of their commitments concerning

economics and politics. This applied particularly to governmental roles, but they were also cautious about professional pastors and priests. In other ways, however, Anabaptists embraced the breadth of calling promoted by sixteenth-century Reformers such as Martin Luther and John Calvin, what we have labeled *vocation*. Their cautions can encourage us to consider ethical and theological dimensions involved in the choice of job and profession.

One area of concern involved Luther's confidence in the "orders of creation," the concept that God has established certain social domains, such as the family, the state, the church, and the economy.[105] Since these were set by society rather than established by the Bible, Anabaptists were suspicious that the concept did not allow for enough critique by Scripture, and especially Jesus' teaching. The kingdom preached by Jesus was upside-down, and those following Jesus should expect things to be in some ways different than what exists in the surrounding culture. Luther, in contrast, argued that even feelings of revulsion at one's work were likely temptations of the devil to keep one away from God's appointment.

Anabaptists were especially wary of professions that involved coercion or violence, and they resisted standard concepts of private ownership in pursuit of arrangements that provided more economic justice. They felt no responsibility to support the structures of their culture, including those involving economics. As they advocated for the poor, they became a threat, as also when they refused to baptize their babies as an entrance ritual into national citizenship.

Some have interpreted such attitudes as part of a deliberate withdrawal from society, but others believe that these Christians began to be ostracized and therefore had fewer options to be involved. While they accepted the biblical teaching that the government was divinely instituted, their conviction was that respect and not obedience was due to magistrates because their true citizenship and true loyalty were to Jesus' kingdom. Some leaders allowed for limited participation in political roles, while others excluded them completely.

Anabaptists saw their economic and ethical lives as indivisible from their spiritual existence.[106] They refused to charge interest on loans to other Christians, a practice of other Christian groups as well, but one that gradually wore down over time. Other than marketing their own crafts, Anabaptists discouraged any form of trade or commerce. Menno Simons cited Ecclesiasticus 26:29–27:3 in this regard (the life of commerce is almost inevitably *sinful*), though in that same apocryphal book (also known as Sirach) he apparently ignored 11:20-21, which urges righteous persons to trust the Lord while *staying* at their jobs.

Anabaptists were concerned not to charge more than a just amount and believed that it was easy to take advantage of people, in effect becoming a thief. Likewise, no one should buy something at a low price and sell it for profit at a higher price. Concern was also expressed for marketing things that promoted pride, ostentation, or vanity. Graber Miller cites historian C. Arnold Snyder who concluded, "[T]here were to be no Swiss Brethren, Hutterite, or Mennonite financiers or entrepreneurs!"[107] Graber Miller urges that, however we disagree with the specific conclusions of the early Anabaptists, we take seriously their concern for the ways in which our involvements exploit or do violence to others rather than bring blessing.

As he traces the descendants of this group of Christians, Graber Miller notes several trends. First, they tended to locate in rural communities because they believed that it would be difficult to maintain their convictions in the cities. As such, they were actual or quasi-owners and had no experience punching a time clock or working with little control over the products of labor. Second, when they left the farm and rural communities, they tended to enter service professions, such as the medical field and education. In the last sixty years, new trends have developed among such groups, including the influx of women into the workforce, the resulting two-income family, and a tremendous broadening of the types of jobs and professions within the believing community. These changes were increasingly "blessed" by leadership, especially by leaders of Mennonite educational institutions. There remains a

general ambivalence in some areas concerning those in ministry, whether professionalism is appropriate or not, and in the
arts, which do not fit a pragmatic attitude toward work.

In his concluding two chapters, Graber Miller explores a
possible Anabaptist approach to vocation. Several elements are
worth highlighting as a special contribution from this particular Christian community:

1. *Calling should be understood primarily and fundamentally as
    being a follower of Jesus Christ.* This means that whatever vo-
    cation or secondary sense of God's direction we pursue, it
    should be tested by its faithfulness to the life and teachings
    of Jesus and discipleship. This is true in both individual
    and corporate dimensions.
2. *A commitment to being Jesus' disciples ought to shape and trans-
    form occupational, business, and professional roles.* We must
    always be asking how our professional roles enhance the
    life of disciples and our task of serving God's kingdom.
3. The *primary content of our vocation* as disciples of Jesus
    Christ is to work at bringing *healing and reconciliation* in the
    midst of God's good and groaning world.

The Unfinished Shakespeare Play

Times of great drama and courageous action can be inspiring.
For most of us, however, the practice of living our calling
faithfully will be a matter of daily and smaller choices. Those
choices prepare us for the times of higher stakes and higher
demands.

N. T. Wright has proposed a kind of parable to help us put
into perspective God's collective call on our lives.[108] Imagine,
he proposes, that a formerly unknown play by William Shakespeare is unearthed. There is initially much excitement. Then it
is realized that only four of the original five acts have been
recovered, that most of the fifth act is missing. What to do?
Should someone try to complete the fifth act? What single
playwright is the equal of Shakespeare? Then a plan is suggested. The key roles will be given to highly trained, sensitive, and
experienced Shakespearian actors who will immerse themselves in the first four acts as well as in the language and

culture of Shakespeare and his time. When they are ready, this troupe will develop the fifth act for themselves, and then perform the complete play. In this scenario, the authority for the play would reside in the first four acts, as well as in what is known about Shakespeare and his other plays. The fifth act would develop and bring to resolution the themes already established in those acts according to the values and tendencies of Shakespeare as playwright.

Wright wants to help us see how the situation of followers of Jesus is similar to that of the actors in this story. Such followers have been given an unfinished story, found most importantly in the Bible, but also in what is known of Christian history elsewhere. Christians work together like the actors to continue God's work in the world, according to the themes already introduced in Scripture and according to the character of the God we know and are coming to know more completely. The acts in the Bible could be presented something like this:

- Act I: Creation
- Act II: Human Disobedience and Loss of Paradise
- Act III: Redemption Begins: The People of Israel
- Act IV: Redemption's Center: Jesus' Life and Teachings
- Act V: New Creation Begins: The Church
  - o   Scene 1: The book of Acts and NT letters
  - o   Scenes 2, 3, 4, …. Ongoing Christian History, including today!
  - o   Scene ? Jesus Returns, New Creation Fulfilled, New Life Begun (see OT prophets, the Book of Revelation)

While we know that God will bring everything to completion according to a plan beyond our comprehension, Wright's parable suggests that the specific scenes of God's drama are not yet developed, at least not in detail. Believers need to study the Bible in order to know better what God intends for us to do (see discussion of story-formed community in ch. 3). Scripture finds its most significant function as it is respected and obeyed in community. The parable shows how Scripture really has authority only as it is performed, that is, put into action.

We need to learn to know God better so that we can do things according to God's character. And, unlike the Shakespearian actors, we have the gift of the Holy Spirit who can guide us, lead us into all truth, and empower us to live out what we need to do.

Our final chapter considers the challenge to carry out our mission, and the opportunity to receive as we give of ourselves to others.

Questions for Reflection and Discussion
1. How does faith in your "ultimate concern" relate to your job or profession?
2. Which "Job and Vocation" model is closest to your own or the one you anticipate?
3. If you have experienced any of the "dualities," indicate which one or ones and describe your experience.
4. Do any of the three emphases of the Anabaptist approach to vocation seem especially important to consider? If so, which and why?
5. What is your reaction to the unfinished Shakespeare play parable? Does this leave the future too wide open? How would you explain the role of Jesus' followers in living faithfully as part of God's mission in the world until Jesus returns?
6. How do the experiences that make up your immediate calling (current tasks) fit into the other two callings (the primary call of relationship to God and secondary call or vocation)?

Suggestions for Further Reading
Keith Graber Miller, *Living Faith: Embracing God's Callings*. Telford, PA: Cascadia, 2012.

Miroslav Volf, *Work in the Spirit: Toward a Theology of Work*. New York: Oxford University Press, 1991.

CHAPTER 14

Will You Accept It?

The story of the prophet Jonah is an excellent one to ponder for several reasons: it has great drama, it is all about receiving a call from God, and it has to do with engaging an entire culture, its values, and its history. This tale is one of the better-known accounts in the Old Testament. Who can forget the story of a reluctant prophet who runs frantically in the opposite direction when called by God? Many have likely felt that kind of panic when confronted with something they did not want to do. And who can forget the drama of being swallowed by a giant fish, yet surviving when spit back on the shore? Yes, we say, much better to obey God than to let the scary Big Guy in the Sky toy with us like playthings in the midst of a vast ocean or anywhere else.

When we look more closely at these slim four chapters in the Bible, however, our initial impressions—or the impressions conveyed to us by Sunday school versions—become seriously challenged. For one thing, the synopsis above does a poor job of accounting for what happens in the four chapters. For example, the fish is only mentioned in two verses, and only plays a role at all in the second chapter. The second chapter is actually devoted to worship, Jonah praying to God. And his prayer is not, as we might expect, praying for mercy, but *thanking* God for being delivered. The final chapter seems like a particular waste: Jonah (finally) has given the message God asked him to give, and the people repented, so why do we need chapter 4?

When puzzles like this arise in our study of the Bible, we can be confident that a closer look will be rewarding, and such is the case here. I must note, first of all, what a great story of irony this is. Most strikingly, the prophet Jonah—whom we initially would have every reason to expect to be obedient to God—is the prime example of *disobedience* in the book. Everyone and everything else here, when challenged regarding God's instructions, complies completely. This is true from pagan sailors, to major storms on the sea, to a giant fish, to the wicked people of Nineveh, to a magnificent plant, and a ravenous worm! So complying with God's wishes is a repeated motif through the story.

But the reason Jonah is worth thinking about here is related to the prophet himself. We discover in Jonah 4 his own explanation for why he fled from God at the outset. It wasn't, as we might have assumed, because he had other things he would rather have done, or because it was daunting to go to the big, bad city of Nineveh. Rather, it was because he knew God was merciful, and was afraid this mercy would extend to the enemy Assyrians in Nineveh. And this provides the reason for the final chapter, a chapter everyone needs who is concerned with following God faithfully. For the whole chapter here helps us to see how much God cares about Jonah, his servant, and not just about Nineveh. We realize that God has given this assignment to Jonah not just for the benefit of the Ninevites. The assignment is also for the benefit of this prophet who cannot open his heart to love his enemy, and who is so afraid that God might actually love them. So despite their repentance, he waits outside the city, hoping for a show of fire and brimstone that will signal the destruction of so many lives.

So God gives Jonah a lesson. As he sits in the sun, God causes a plant to grow up and give him shade. But then a worm eats the plant and causes it to die. Jonah, who was so happy about the shade, is now deeply angry at its loss. "And should I not have concern about the great city of Nineveh," asks God, ". . . more than a hundred and twenty thousand people . . . and also many animals?" (Jon. 4:11). And there the book ends. We never hear Jonah's answer to this question. Perhaps you and I as readers are expected to feel the weight of that question as well. Do we love our enemies? Do we rejoice over God's love for them as well as God's love for us?

So the point: God was as concerned for change in Jonah as for change in the Ninevites. As Jonah responded to God's call, God was able to work in the life of the prophet as well. This awareness can help us in at least two ways. First, as we give, we receive, just as Jesus said (Luke 6:38). God loves us just as much as the people to whom we are sent and wants to provide for us. Second, it can help us set aside any subtle and sub-merged self-congratulations as we carry out acts of love and service for others. We are just as needy, sometimes more. This should humble us, which means, as we recognize the truth, there is no room for thinking of ourselves as superior to any-one else.

What We Do, Who We Become

In connection with our examination of vocation, the story of Jonah is wonderful and important. We see once again that God delights in working through people, in calling people to carry out the divine mission on behalf of all creation. It is encourag-ing again to see that God uses the weak and imperfect, and that there is something good for us in carrying out our role in this project that Jesus called the kingdom of God. Here we will re-flect just briefly on another lesson from this story, the change God sought to happen in Jonah.

We have considered previously the importance of commu-nities for shaping people in noble and virtuous ways, such as we saw illustrated in the courageous communities of Le Chambon, France, and Timisoara, Romania. Communities can also shape us in negative ways, of course, and from Jonah's story we can sense that despite his role as God's prophet, he had been nurtured into attitudes and orientations of frustration and hatred toward the violent and pagan Assyrians. God wanted to change Jonah, and not just in his willingness to carry out an assignment. Rather, God wanted Jonah to develop an internal virtue that could be called compassion even toward those who were his enemies.

Perhaps we more easily remember the instructions of Jesus that emphasize what we *do*, such as the Golden Rule (do to others what you would have them do to you, Matt. 7:12), and the two great commandments to love God and love our neighbor (Matt. 22:36-40). Yet the Beatitudes, that listing of those who are blessed that is given by Jesus in Matthew 5:1-12, are a rich collection of both action-oriented characteristics, such as peacemaking, and virtue-oriented traits, such as meekness and purity. In fact, Jesus cautions against doing the right things for the wrong reasons in his teaching concerning giving, prayer, and fasting (Matt. 6:1-18).

Elsewhere in the Bible we also find a concern for *being* as well as doing, such as the call to be transformed from the patterns of this world to the mind of Christ (Rom. 12:1-2). It would not be so healthy to respond to this awareness about virtue by constantly examining our motives for what we do, though that can be helpful from time to time. Rather, it is important to put into practice those things that will most likely cultivate the virtues of Christlikeness in us, virtues such as the fruit of the Spirit mentioned by Paul in Galatians 5:22-23.

Returning to our analogy given in chapter 9, virtues concern the internal workings of the ship. The other two issues — ships cruising together and reaching the right destination — are getting along with people and the ultimate goal of humanity.

Virtues for Vocation

Gordon Smith has highlighted five virtues that are particularly important for our vocations.[109] On the sublime level, these are virtues that fill our service of God by serving others with joy and satisfaction. On the more mundane level, they make it much more likely that we will attain and keep our jobs. Each of them also has a distortion that needs to be noted.

Excellence is something that all Christians need to practice and internalize. As the Message version puts it,

> Servants, . . . don't just do the minimum that will get you by. Do your best. Work from the heart for your real Master, for God. . . . The sullen servant who does shoddy work will be held responsible. Being Christian doesn't cover up bad work. (Col. 3:22-25)

And as Martin Luther King Jr. expressed it,

> Even if it falls your lot to be a street sweeper, go on out and sweep streets like Michelangelo painted pictures; sweep streets like Handel and Beethoven composed music; sweep streets like Shakespeare wrote poetry; sweep streets so well that all the hosts of heaven and earth will have to pause and say, "Here lived a great street sweeper who swept his job well."[110]

However, distortions of a focus on excellence include the traps of perfectionism, materialism, and caring too much what others think compared to what God thinks of our work. An antidote is to relax in the grace that God offers us, our knowledge that we are accepted through no merit of our own.

A second vocation virtue is *truth*, integrity, meaning what we say and saying what we mean. There are few characteristics that make us more valued than the confidence others can have that we are people of honesty. At the same time, we need the courage to speak truth when doing so could place us at odds with our employer or others who have power over us.

> . . . by the open statement of truth we commend ourselves to the conscience of everyone . . . (2 Cor. 2:17 NRSV)

A distortion of this virtue is that it can become bigotry, including the desire to silence others, something the world has plenty of already. What we need is teachableness combined with a confidence that God's truth will win out despite the threat of lies and falsehood around us.

A third important virtue is *diligence*, as we find in this text:

> Be diligent to present yourself approved to God, a worker who doesn't need to be ashamed . . . . [P]ersist in [your assignment] whether convenient or not (2 Tim. 2:15; 4:2 HCSB)

Diligence means hard work, applying oneself thoroughly, and responsibly staying on task. There are two major distortions involving diligence. One, no surprise, is exhaustion, confusing hectic activity with diligence or confusing work addiction with diligence. The second is being confused into thinking that your vocation is to make money. Of course, money can be a gift you provide for projects of God's kingdom, but your vocation will always be something more. To counter these tendencies, we need a Sabbath mindset that trusts God to manage the world.

A fourth important virtue is *generosity*, valuing human beings as having eternal worth so that sharing of oneself is never wasted. This includes supporting one's coworkers, and it also means sharing of oneself in generous service to customers. Jesus modeled generosity by serving and giving "his life as a ransom for many" (Mark 10:45). He also made the following promise:

> Give, and it will be given to you. A good measure, pressed down, shaken together and running over, will be poured into your lap. For with the measure you use, it will be measured to you. (Luke 6:38)

The distortions of generosity are related to overcommitment: creating dependence of others upon us, sometimes because we have developed a "Messiah complex" and need others to need us; neglect of our family and others for whom we are primarily responsible; and omitting justice (the rights of others). Our generosity must be for equipping others so that they can be generous themselves, and not so that they fall into the trap of dysfunctional self-absorption. Antidotes to these distortions include learning to say "no" to some requests, and allowing oneself to be served, just as Jesus did (Luke 7:36-50; John 12:1-8).

Before addressing Gordon Smith's final point, I want to add a virtue to his list: *endurance*. We need endurance as we live our vocation for a variety of reasons. It is necessary when we are waiting to be employed; we need it when working a job in order to stay alive or without a meaningful sense of serving others; we need endurance when we are underpaid or experience other forms of unappreciation; we need it when we are doing our vocation, but it doesn't seem to be going well though we don't know why; and we need endurance when everything seems to be going well, and we wonder if it will keep going that way. On several occasions Jesus is recorded saying that the one who "endures to the end will be saved" (Matt. 10:22; 24:13;

Mark 13:13 NRSV), reflecting the future dimension of God's salvation. The major distortion of endurance is stubbornness. The antidote comes primarily in two areas: reminders that God will bring the harvest (Gal. 6:9), and time spent in prayer (Luke 18:1).

The final quality that Smith admonishes is **Sabbath**, not so much a virtue but a discipline that keeps virtues healthy. He urges us to establish a life rhythm of work and leisure, prayer and action, worship and service. The distortion is sloth: enjoying times of break so much that we want them all the time. The antidote is in the rhythms to which Smith points us, and cultivating gratitude for both work and Sabbath.

Making one day a special time of rest and worship was central to the faith of Israel where it is found among the Ten Commandments (Exod. 20:8-11; Deut. 5:12-15). One of the best explanations for celebrating this day comes from Clarence Hiebert. He urges that we make sure we have accomplished each of the four "Ah's" for a satisfying Sabbath day:

a.   The "ah" of *rest*. Stop working. Take a break. Let your body and mind recover from a week of work.
b.   The "ah" (or awe) of *worship*. Spend time honoring God, loving God, enjoying God.
c.   The "ah" of *fellowship*. Spend time with brothers and sisters in Christ in worship, prayer, singing, study, laughter, and encouragement.
d.   The "ah" of *insight*. Allow your mind to be stimulated, through the pastor's sermon, through Christian education at church, through a book or other input.

A Final Word about Virtue. There are, of course, many other virtues that God wants to build into our lives, such as anger at injustice, joy when truth prevails, and compassion on those who are suffering. As virtues develop in our lives, through the help of pastors and mentors, they shape the character of our vocation. They determine what kind of lawyer, engineer, coach, educator, carpenter, lab technician, artist, or therapist we will become. And just how those jobs and professions will serve the goals and purposes of God's kingdom.

An Important Warning

Before concluding, you should hear a warning about vocation. This warning may sound odd, especially in a book that is focused on helping you be as clear about and as motivated for your vocation as possible. The warning is this, that there may be no competitor against the *primary calling*—to love and serve God with our whole hearts and love God's people—as great as the *secondary calling*, that vocation and mission to which God is directing our lives!

How can this be? It would seem that to find one's vocation, and to give oneself fully to that area of service would necessarily draw one closer to God and God's people. And that is the way it should be. But we can never take this for granted. As noted above, Jesus warned about the spiritual disciplines of prayer, giving to the poor, and fasting that it is subtly possible to do the right things for the wrong reasons. Jesus particularly highlighted the motivation of being seen and praised by others (Matt. 6:1-18).

The devil's temptations of Jesus in the wilderness come on the cusp of his mission (Matt. 4:1-11; Luke 4:1-13). When the devil takes Jesus to the pinnacle of the temple and invites him to jump, Jesus is tempted to do something for the praise of people, an extension of the concern he described in Matthew 6. This would also have been a shortcut for the appropriate fame he would achieve by following his true calling at the appropriate time. When the devil urges Jesus to turn stones into bread, he appeals to his need for physical sustenance, but also for security. This would also have been a shortcut for the time when he would appropriately provide food for others and himself. When the devil urges Jesus to fall down and worship him, he offers him power. This would have been a shortcut for the power Jesus would receive from the Holy Spirit upon emerging from this time of testing (Luke 4:14).

These are all challenges to the character and principles of Jesus' ministry, and to each Jesus quotes Scripture (all from Deuteronomy). And Jesus rejects the challenges on the basis of his relationship with God, which must always come first: live by the words that come from God (Deut. 8:3), worship the Lord alone (Deut. 6:13), and do not put the Lord to the test (Deut.

6:16). Doubtless these are not the only aspects involved with our vocation that can draw us from our first love. We must beware of the thrill of satisfaction that comes from a job well done, and of the satisfaction of helping people with genuine needs. These experiences become holy as we turn them into expressions of joy and gratitude to the God who made us, loves us, and requires us to love our Maker with all our being (Deut. 6:4-5). Otherwise one's mission, like anything else, can actually become an idol that subtly replaces God.

For the second of the two great commandments—love your neighbor as yourself—though it can never be disconnected from the first, is always the *second* commandment. The first remains: you must "love the Lord your God with all your heart and with all your soul and with all your mind and with all your strength" (Mark 12:28-31). Note how Jesus asks the question to Peter, "[D]o you love me more than these?" where *these* can be a fill-in-the-blank, *anything* else (John 21:15-19). But certainly in the context of Jesus assigning Peter his vocation to "feed my sheep," we must recognize that all of our service needs to find its perspective and motivation within our first love for God (Rev. 2:4). (For some suggestions on keeping the primary calling *primary*, see Appendix B.)

Your Mission: Will You Accept It?
The popular television and movie franchise *Mission: Impossible* presents a motif early in each scenario: a description is given of the task at hand, the desperation of the need, and the unlikelihood of success. In the midst of this presentation, the supervisory voice always intones, "your mission, should you decide to accept it," and then gives a succinct description of the assignment. It is time to pause now and decide whether you will accept your mission, one that is *possible* because God is with you.

We approached the issue of purpose in terms of a life of adventure. To live our call thoughtfully means to take on some challenging questions. We need to review the messages, distortions, and false worldview options of the culture around us, pondering the nature of the faith we place in others and particularly in matters of ultimate concern. We also need to understand how to think ethically and consider a healthy process for ethical deliberation as well as to evaluate how from within our worldview to engage the culture around us.

Our journey in this book uncovered a Christian approach to vocation that is part of God's Design (SCAR) in the world: salvation, community, abundant life, and relationship with God, four themes that emerge from a central concern to love God and love our neighbor. We considered three callings: the primary call, to relate with God by placing oneself under God's direction and to join God's community; the secondary call, the vocation for which we are created and shaped; and the immediate call, the individual tasks we face each day. The vocation, or specific mission, for each person will reflect a distinctive mix of the Creation Mandate (rule over and care for all creation) and the Great Commission (make disciples of Jesus). This will play out in one of five relationships between our job or profession and our vocation. In the process of *doing* our mission, God will transform our *being* through characteristics called virtues, and help us avoid traps of false identity.

We also considered a process through which our sense of vocation could become more clear. Jesus taught us through the parable of the master and servants that we have abilities, opportunities, and resources for our vocation. Reflecting on that combination, along with some other determinations of our shape, can help us to find those next steps for the mission to which we are called. We can aim for the intersection of our deep gladness and the world's deep hunger.

If we want to avoid being like Warren Schmidt, we will need to be open to hearing a call not unlike that of Jonah. Though it was something Jonah was not eager to hear, in the process he was challenged to face up to himself and had opportunity to change for the better. Because we are on adventure, we will not know exactly what is ahead. We may not be able to have the job or profession we most want or that seems most suitable for us. Even if we enjoy our profession, we may experience hard times. We will likely make mistakes; others may do us wrong. In short, God's calling is not the American Dream. We are called to obey God whether it is something we enjoy or not. The goal is not focused on us, but on God's purposes in the world.

It is encouraging to know we are not alone on this journey but travel with others, some of whom align with our world-view and others who do not. We will need to decide with whom to partner and how to engage the culture around us as we bring our vocation together with our job and profession. We can remember that God promises us eternal joy and, despite hardships, that joy begins now!

May you find that joy as well as challenge in the adventure ahead.

Questions for Reflection and Discussion
1. Have you accepted your primary calling? If you are not committed and submitted to the God of Christian faith, to whom or what does your commitment lie?
2. Have you been able to identify your vocation? Or do you at least have an idea for the next step? Are you ready or have you committed yourself to following that vocation and/or that next step?
3. Consider the story of Jonah. Are there ways God is seeking to bless your life as you serve others? Are there ways you need to change for that to happen?
4. How might you allow important virtues to be cultivated in your own life and in the lives of others you care about?
5. What areas of life are a current or potential threat to loving God with all that you are?
6. Is there a faith community, pastor, and/or mentor who can help you continue to grow in the virtues of life?
7. Are you ready to accept your mission? Why or why not?

Suggestions for Further Reading
Douglas B. Miller, "Will Jonah Be Saved?" in *Beautiful upon the Mountains: Biblical Essays on Mission, Peace, and the Reign of God*, 77-98. Elkhart, IN: Institute of Mennonite Studies, 2003.

Henri J. M. Nouwen, *The Wounded Healer*. New York: Image, 1979.

Eugene H. Peterson, *Working the Angles: The Shape of Pastoral Ministry*. Grand Rapids, MI: Eerdmans, 1987.

A Personal Mission Statement

A personal mission statement helps you reflect on your future plans and goals, to put them in perspective, and to consider how best to achieve them.[111]

- A Mission Statement is a declaration of life purpose.
- For the Christian, it is a statement of what a person or group has determined is God's specific "call" and responsibility for their lives. It is the area of God's kingdom work for which they have received gifts, grace, and direction.
- Those who do not consider themselves religious, or have adopted a different worldview, may want to think in terms of what provides purpose or meaning in life.
- Note: This is not necessarily a blueprint for the rest of your life. It is a statement of (a) the best of what you know now, and (b) your intentions for the next step(s) in your life.

Benefits of having a mission statement include the following:

- It helps us focus our lives in terms of our relationships with friends, family, and the folks we go to church with.
- It helps us with important life choices, including how we use our time and money, where we live (both part of the world and specific neighborhood), what profession and job we take, and even whom we might marry.
- And it helps us know why we should get up in the morning.

The following paragraphs give a few suggestions for a process that could result in formulating a personal mission statement.

Some Basic Assumptions

This process is based on the assumption that, at any given time, there is a purpose or "calling" for each person. Another assumption is that we can start to make sense of this purpose, or that God wants to make clear to each person how they can best fulfill a God-inspired mission in their life. Finally, this process assumes that, just as nature abhors a vacuum, if we aren't intentional about setting a definite focus for our lives, other forces will step in to set the direction for our lives. Therefore, it is important to be clear and intentional about our discernment of call or purpose.

How to Hear a Call

A sense of call or purpose can come in a variety of ways. As noted in chapter 3, some of the common approaches that people use to discern this direction have had mixed results. The process proposed below reflects time-tested ways that people have used to get clarity in this area. It borrows from a process used by Quaker Christians called "listening for clearness." To summarize, clarity can come to us through three venues:

(1) Through *our own lives*. Quaker author Parker Palmer encourages us "to listen to what our lives are saying *and* take notes on it, lest we forget our own truth or deny that we ever heard it."[112] See the SHAPE elements below.
(2) Through the *Scriptures and other texts*. These can give us clues to our own gifts and calling.
(3) Through the *lives of others*. Good ideas come from other people, and you may discern God speaking to you in this way. This can happen either directly or when someone lives in a way that inspires us to emulate. It is also important to test the ideas we get from items 1 and 2 above with friends and those who are wise.

Here are some details concerning the elements of SHAPE, a way of exploring the first venue indicated above.

Successes and Struggles: Start by thinking of projects you have been part of, either in a group or on your own. What went particularly well? What triumphs were exciting for you? What role or roles did you play? Also consider failures, "broken places," and other aspects of your life that have not gone so well. Struggles are often painful, but some-times they provide insight into our life direction.

Heart: These are your passions, the things that get you emo-tionally energized. Consider reflecting on these two areas to see what memories get you excited or disturbed: (a) the needs of other people, and (b) specific hopes and "dreams"—things in your imagination. These two may align, as Frederick Buechner suggests, "The place God calls you to is the place where your deep gladness and the world's deep hunger meet."[113] Part of wisdom is to realize you can't do it all, and for that reason, the world's needs in themselves do not determine your call.

Abilities: These are, first of all, your so-called "natural" talents and also your skills, the things you are good at. Usually, other people notice these things and may have told you so. Or you may take an inventory, such as Strengths Finder. Second, the Bible tells us that the Holy Spirit gives differ-ent abilities to followers of Jesus so that Christians are equipped to complement one another while doing God's work. These are often called "spiritual gifts." The Bible lists some of these in Romans 12:3-8 and 1 Corinthians 12:4-11.

Personality: We have ways of describing personalities fairly casually—whether thinking or feeling is stronger for you, whether you like routine or spontaneity, whether you re-charge alone or with people, and so on. But some helpful personality tests have been developed that can give further insight, such as the Four Temperaments Analysis and the Myers-Briggs Type Indicator.[114]

Experience: Finally, there may be other things in your back-ground. You may wish to focus on family, education or other training, ministry, times of prayer, special events, or anything else that has not been addressed by the above items. Do any of these provide a certain motivation that is significant for you? Review of your life may take courage, but all these elements of SHAPE can provide clues to your life purpose.

For two sample mission statements, see chapter 3 above.

Organizing Your Life around Worship

In our time it is a radical act to figure out priorities and live by them. Hear how Jesus responded to such questions:

> One of the teachers of the law came and heard them debating. Noticing that Jesus had given them a good answer, he asked him, "Of all the commandments, which is the most important?" [29] "The most important one," answered Jesus, "is this: 'Hear, O Israel: The Lord our God, the Lord is one. [30] Love the Lord your God with all your heart and with all your soul and with all your mind and with all your strength.' [31] The second is this: 'Love your neighbor as yourself.' There is no commandment greater than these." (Mark 12:28-31)

One of the dangerous ironies of identifying and committing to one's secondary calling (vocation) is that it can pose a serious threat to one's primary calling, that is, to your relationship with God's people and to God, especially to loving and knowing God as the highest priority of your life. C. S. Lewis explains it this way:

> God's claim is infinite and inexorable. You can refuse it, or you can begin to try to grant it. There is no middle way. Yet in spite of this it is clear that Christianity does not exclude any of the ordinary human activities. . . . The solution of this paradox is, of course, well known to you. "Whether ye eat or drink or whatsoever ye do, do all to the glory of God" [1 Cor. 10:31]. All our merely natural activities will be accepted, if they are offered to God, even the humblest, and all of them, even the noblest, will be sinful if they are not.[115]

What follows are some suggestions for helping to keep the primary calling primary, tested across time and various cultures.

Develop a Routine

The term *routine* has taken on the connotation of something that is dull and uninspiring. However, as used here, it is a pattern that can keep us spiritually alive with aspects of our lives in the proper perspective. In that way it is like the routines of breathing, eating, and sleeping. We need such patterns to be healthy. Here are a few ideas:

1. *Seven-Minute Quiet Time.* Many people have found it extremely helpful to spend some time each day "in God's presence," that is, a time set aside for prayer, reflection, and often reading the Bible. Make it regular if possible, whether it fits best for you in the morning, in the evening, or some other time. Here is a simple model that requires only seven minutes and, of course, can be expanded much beyond that if you wish. It begins with a disarming question, "Can you get quiet with God for seven minutes today?" Some days that might not be possible, but consider that most of the time this is possible and valuable. Here's an idea to help it work.

   a. Read and reflect on the Bible for four minutes. Read until something sticks, something you can think about for a while.

   b. Pray for three minutes in these areas of focus (ACTS): Adoration (say some words of praise to God), Cry out (express yourself emotionally, e.g., confession, pain), Thanks (say thank you for the good things), and Supplication (ask for what you need for yourself and for others)

2. *Sabbath.* The discipline of Sabbath for oneself, one's family, and one's business means to establish a rhythm of work and leisure, prayer and action, worship and service that involves making one day of the week set apart. See the discussion of Sabbath in chapter 12 above.

3. *Spiritual Disciplines.* Learn to practice one or more of the disciplines that have been carried on by Christians for centuries. The above two items are a great way to get started. Then consider the items below.

Spiritual Disciplines: What Are They?
Christians have learned that certain practices can be extremely helpful to keep us focused, strengthened, growing in our faith, and productive for God's call on our lives. Here are some of them, with a brief description. Consider how to practice these alone and also with others. Richard Foster says it well, "The purpose of the Disciplines is freedom. Our aim is the freedom, not the Discipline. The moment we make the Discipline our central focus we will turn it into law and lose the corresponding freedom."[116]

1. *Prayer*. Spending time with God, talking and listening. Prayer dimensions include praise, thanksgiving, lament, petition, and confession. Prayers may be silent, vocal, or written in a journal.
2. *Meditation*. An exercise in reflection upon God, God's instructions, Scripture, or other aspects of faith.
3. *Fasting*. Ceasing to participate in food or something else in one's normal routine for the purpose of special focus and prayer.
4. *Scripture*. Memorization, study, and/or meditation upon portions of the Bible.
5. *Study*. A plan of learning in order to grow in faith.
6. *Simplicity*. An inward reality of focus and unity that results in an outward lifestyle that puts less emphasis on material possessions and special experiences.
7. *Solitude and Silence*. Time spent away from noise and crowds.
8. *Submission*. Setting aside the need to have one's own way by serving under the direction of another.
9. *Service*. A special focus on helping to meet the needs of others. Here is an opportunity to make your vocation an act of worship, doing it for God out of gratitude for all God has done for you.
10. *Worship*. In a sense, all of the above, and hopefully all we do, can be an act of honoring and loving God that could be called worship. As a discipline, it can refer to times of corporate or individual prayer, song, reflection on Scripture,

and other matters that are focused on being a delight to God. According to Jesus (John 4:23), God seeks people to worship in spirit and truth.

Suggestions for Further Reading

Richard Foster, *Celebration of Discipline*. San Francisco, CA: Harper and Row, 1978.

Gordon MacDonald, *Ordering Your Private World*, rev. ed. Nashville, TN: Thomas Nelson, 2003.

Donald S. Whitney, *Spiritual Disciplines for the Christian Life*. Colorado Springs, CO: NavPress, 1991.

Dallas Willard, *The Spirit of the Disciplines*. San Francisco, CA: Harper and Row, 1989.

Notes

[1] *Never Cry Wolf*, Walt Disney pictures, 1983, based on the book by Farley Mowat (Atlantic–Little, Brown, 1963).

[2] The NIV (2011) Bible translation is used unless otherwise indicated.

[3] *The Fellowship of the Ring*, New Line Cinema, 2001.

[4] James W. Sire, *Naming the Elephant: Worldview as a Concept,* 2nd ed. (Downers Grove, IL: InterVarsity, 2015), 141.

[5] Sire, *Naming the Elephant,* 14.

[6] Most of these are discussed in James W. Sire, *The Universe Next Door: A Basic Worldview Catalog,* 5th ed. (Downers Grove, IL: InterVarsity, 2009), chs. 2–10. Also see Peter Kreeft, *The Journey: A Spiritual Roadmap for Modern Pilgrims* (Downers Grove, IL: InterVarsity, 1996).

[7] Steve Wilkens and Mark Sanford argue that partial worldviews are just as significant as the major ones in our time. In practice, that is, as we live our lives, these perspectives overlap, sharing elements with each other. Thus, each person may participate in several at once. So in their discussion of worldviews, Wilkens and Sanford include the following: Individualism, Consumerism, Nationalism, Moral Relativism, Postmodern Tribalism, and Salvation by Therapy, among others. Steve Wilkens and Mark L. Sanford, *Hidden Worldviews: Eight Cultural Stories that Shape Our Lives* (Downers Grove, IL: InterVarsity, 2009).

[8] Brian J. Walsh and J. Richard Middleton, *The Transforming Vision: Shaping a Christian Worldview* (Downers Grove, IL: InterVarsity, 1984), ch. 2; the fifth question is added by N. T. Wright, *Jesus and the Victory of God* (London: SPCK, 1996), 443, 467–72.

[9] Gordon T. Smith, *Courage and Calling,* 1st ed. (Downers Grove, IL: InterVarsity, 1999), 15–20.

[10] Gordon T. Smith, *Courage and Calling,* 2nd ed. (Downers Grove, IL: InterVarsity, 2011), 128–32.

[11] The power of metaphors for influencing how we understand ourselves is insightfully explained in George Lakoff and Mark Johnson, *Metaphors We Live By,* 2nd ed. (Chicago: University of Chicago Press, 2003). For the significance of identity on a corporate and national

scale, see Richard T. Hughs, *Myths America Lives By* (Urbana and Chicago: University of Illinois Press, 2004).

[12] Smith, *Courage and Calling*, 2nd ed., 9–10.

[13] Parker Palmer, *Let Your Life Speak* (San Francisco, CA: Jossey-Bass, 2000), 6.

[14] The basic idea of the SHAPE acronym, developed differently here, is found in Rick Warren, *The Purpose Driven Life* (Grand Rapids, MI: Zondervan, 2002), 234–39.

[15] Christine and Tom Sine, *Living on Purpose: Finding God's Best for Your Life* (Grand Rapids, MI: Baker, 2002), 77–89.

[16] Similarly later, John Calvin; see his *Institutes of the Christian Religion*, I, v, 14.

[17] Avery Dulles, "The Meaning of Faith Considered in Relationship to Justice," in *The Faith That Does Justice: Examining the Christian Sources for Social Change*, ed. John C. Haughey (New York: Paulist, 1977), 14–22.

[18] Dulles, 22–31.

[19] Dulles, 32–44.

[20] For a helpful presentation of these issues, see Thomas H. Groome, *Christian Religious Education: Sharing Our Story and Vision* (San Francisco, CA: Harper & Row, 1980), 56–69.

[21] Groome, 61.

[22] Groome, 61–62.

[23] Note Jesus' criticism of Thomas's failure to accept the testimony of reliable witnesses that he had actually risen from the dead. The reader of John's Gospel similarly considers its testimony about Jesus (John 20:24–29).

[24] Groome, 65–66.

[25] Augustine, *Tractates on the Gospel of John*, 29. Later, Anselm of Canterbury coined the phrase "faith seeking understanding." For both, the idea is that those who come to faith in God have a restless desire to grow in their understanding, an aspect of increasing in knowledge of and love for God. For Karl Barth, this includes testing the faith practices of the Christian community. See Daniel L. Migliore, *Faith Seeking Understanding: An Introduction to Christian Theology*, 3rd ed. (Grand Rapids, MI: Eerdmans, 2014), 2.

[26] Tristar Pictures, 2015.

[27] Elmer A. Martens, *God's Design*, 4th ed. (Eugene, OR: Wipf & Stock, 2015).

[28] The first three themes overlap with each other, and the fourth intersects with each of the first three. For example, a life cannot be truly abundant without a healthy relationship with God and with other human beings, and restoring those is part of what the Bible means by "salvation."

[29] Douglas B. Miller, *Ecclesiastes,* Believers Church Bible Commentary (Scottdale, PA: Herald, 2010), 226–29, 235–37.

[30] Os Guinness, *The Call: Finding and Fulfilling the Central Purpose of Your Life* (Nashville, TN: Word, 1998), 98.

[31] Daniel Taylor, *Tell Me a Story: The Life-Shaping Power of Our Stories* (St. Paul, MN: Bog Walk, 2001), 5.

[32] Richard Adams, *Watership Down* (London: Rex Collings, 1972).

[33] Howard Jones, *Mutiny on the* Amistad*: The Saga of a Slave Revolt and its Impact on American Abolition, Law, and Diplomacy* (New York: Oxford University Press, 1987).

[34] Thomas B. Leininger, lecture notes "Scripture & Ethics," Regis University, Denver, Colorado. See also Stanley Hauerwas, "A Story-Formed Community: Reflections on *Watership Down,*" in *A Community of Character* (Notre Dame: University of Notre Dame Press, 1981), 9–35.

[35] Robert Banks, *Paul's Idea of Community,* 2nd ed. (Peabody, MA: Hendrickson, 1994), 26–27.

[36] Paul S. Minear, *Images of the Church in the New Testament* (Philadelphia, PA: Westminster, 1960) and adapted from the (Mennonite Brethren) *Confession of Faith: Commentary and Pastoral Application* (Winnipeg, MB: Kindred, 2000), 68–69, 78–79.

[37] Philip P. Hallie, *Lest Innocent Blood Be Shed* (New York: Harper & Row, 1979), 2–3, 4.

[38] Hallie, 10.

[39] Hallie, 20.

[40] Guinness, 97.

[41] Laszlo Tokes and David Porter, *The Fall of Tyrants* (Wheaton, IL: Crossway, 1990).

[42] Tokes and Porter, 3–4.

[43] There are many, including some Christians, who accept evolution as an account of the sequence through which biological life developed while rejecting a reductive Naturalist worldview. For a helpful overview of proposals regarding origins with their worldview implications, see Gerald Rau, *Mapping the Origins Debate* (Downers Grove, IL: InterVarsity, 2012).

[44] John Wisdom, "Gods," in *Classical and Contemporary Readings in the Philosophy of Religion*, ed. John Hick (Engelwood Cliffs, NJ: Prentice-Hall, 1964). The parable was later expanded by Antony Flew to include additional detection devices, but the gardener is never found. Flew later published an account of how he found the gardener: Antony Flew, *There Is a God: How the World's Most Notorious Atheist Changed His Mind* (New York: HarperOne, 2007). See esp. the parable regarding evidence that begins ch. 4.

[45] The story is famously retold in poetic form by John Godfrey Saxe (1816–1887).

[46] Leslie Newbigin, *The Gospel in a Pluralist Society* (Grand Rapids, MI: Eerdmans, 1989), 9–10.

[47] The first stirrings of this philosophical movement are often noted in the seventeenth century. It was characterized by empiricism and the scientific method, and challenged fixed locations of authority, such as the monarchy and the established church.

[48] John Dewey, *Reconstruction in Philosophy* (New York: Henry Holt, 1920), ch. 2.

[49] Robert W. Jenson, "How the World Lost Its Story." *First Things* 36 (October 1993): 19–24. The Jewish Scriptures equal the "Old Testament" of the Christian Bible. The first Christians were Jewish and embraced the same worldview.

[50] N. T. Wright, *Simply Christian: Why Christianity Makes Sense* (San Francisco: HarperCollins, 2006), part 1.

[51] Saint Augustine, *The Confessions; The City of God; On Christian Doctrine* (ed. Mortimer J. Adler and Philip W. Goetz; trans. R. S. Pine-Coffin, et al.; vol. 16, 2nd ed.; Great Books of the Western World; Chicago, IL: Encyclopædia Britannica, 1990), 1.

[52] C. S. Lewis, *Mere Christianity* (New York: Macmillan, 1952), Book II, ch. 3.

[53] Wright, *Simply Christian*, 31.

[54] Lewis explains his understanding of *Sehnsucht* in numerous of his writings, but most notably in his autobiography, *Surprised by Joy* (New York: Harcourt, Brace, and World, 1955), and in the preface to the third edition of his first book after becoming a Christian, *The Pilgrim's Regress*. 3rd ed. (Grand Rapids, MI: Eerdmans, 1943).

[55] G. K. Chesterton, *What's Wrong with the World* (London: Cassell, 1910), part 1, ch. 5.

[56] For portions of this summary, see Parker J. Palmer, *To Know as We Are Known* (San Francisco, CA: Harper & Row, 1983), ch. 4, "What Is Truth?"

[57] Martin B. Copenhaver, *Jesus Is the Question* (Nashville, TN: Abingdon, 2014), 87.

[58] Lewis, *Mere Christianity*, Book II, ch. 3. Lewis dismisses the moral teacher/prophet option on the basis of what he understands to be Jesus' claims to divinity found in the Gospels. He argues that only the fourth option makes sense in light of all the data.

[59] Lewis, *Surprised by Joy*, 228–29.

[60] Peter Kreeft, *A Refutation of Moral Relativism: Interviews with an Absolutist* (San Francisco, CA: Ignatius, 1999), 135–49.

[61] William James, *The Will to Believe and Other Essays in Popular Philosophy* (New York: Dover Publications, 1956), 31.

[62] I am indebted to Ted Grimsrud for this ethical scenario.

[63] Alasdair MacIntyre, *After Virtue: A Study in Moral Theory*, 3rd ed. (Notre Dame, IN: University of Notre Dame Press, 2007), 2.

[64] Christian Smith, et al., *Lost in Transition: The Dark Side of Emerging Adulthood* (New York: Oxford University Press, 2011), 68–69.

[65] Lewis, *Mere Christianity*, Book 3, ch. 1.

[66] Cf. also Mark 12:28-34 and Luke 10:25-28. Note how Micah 6:8 also addresses God and humanity. For an overview of Jewish summaries of Torah, see Amy-Jill Levine, *The Misunderstood Jew: The Church and the Scandal of the Jewish Jesus* (San Francisco, CA: HarperSanFrancisco, 2006), 21–23.

[67] The Wesleyan Quadrilateral is named after the eighteenth-century Methodist leader John Wesley. He proposed four elements for illuminating the truths of Christian faith: Scripture, tradition, experience, and reason. The "hermeneutical spiral" envisions these four interacting with each other through time in the life of believers individually and collectively.

[68] This section owes much to Glen H. Stassen and David P. Gushee, *Kingdom Ethics: Following Jesus in Contemporary Context*, 2nd ed. (Grand Rapids, MI: Eerdmans, 2016), ch. 4, "The Form and Function of Moral Norms."

[69] Lewis, *Mere Christianity*, Book 3, ch. 1.

[70] This is also a prime concern of what is sometimes called "virtue ethics," often associated with the fourth classic type of ethics (contextualism and narrative ethics) and connected with the basic

convictions level of the Stassen-Gushee model. Who we are and what we do are intimately interconnected.

[71] *Mere Christianity*, Book 3, ch. 1.

[72] The description and discussion of *Pleasantville* (New Line Cinema, 1998) draw from a review by Roger Ebert (*Sun Times*, October 1, 1998) and another by Michael O'Sullivan (*Washington Post*, October 23, 1998).

[73] Nicholas Wolterstorff, *Until Justice and Peace Embrace* (Grand Rapids, MI: Eerdmans, 1983), 124. I am indebted to David Faber for this reference and for its application to *Pleasantville*.

[74] This is also ironic because the film fails to recognize a larger reality beyond the individual realities it is urging each viewer to establish.

[75] Perry B. Yoder, *Shalom: The Bible's Word for Salvation, Justice, and Peace* (Newton, KS: Faith and Life, 1987), 10–19.

[76] Wolterstorff, 124. Similarly, Thomas More in *Utopia* advocates that the pursuit of true happiness would affirm traditional morality and the Christian worldview.

[77] Benjamin R. Barber, *Jihad vs. McWorld* (New York: Ballantine, 1995, with 2001 Introduction), xi–xii. The term *disintegral tribalism* refers to the breakdown of tribal consciousness and loyalty because of the encroachment of other cultural systems and loyalties. Fundamentalism is an attitude toward a belief system that emphasizes strict and literal commitment to a set of basic principles.

[78] Barber, xii–xiii.

[79] Tom Sine, *Mustard Seed versus McWorld: Reinventing Life and Faith for the Future* (Grand Rapids, MI: Baker, 1999), 22.

[80] Tom Sine, *The Mustard Seed Conspiracy* (Waco, TX: Word, 1981), 11–12.

[81] Adapted from Sine, *Mustard Seed versus McWorld*, 22–24.

[82] See especially Glen H. Stassen, D. M. Yeager, and John Howard Yoder, *Authentic Transformation: A New Vision of Christ and Culture* (Nashville, TN: Abingdon, 1996). Two helpful recent studies are Craig A. Carter, *Rethinking* Christ and Culture*: A Post-Christendom Perspective* (Grand Rapids, MI: Brazos, 2006), and D. A. Carson, *Christ and Culture Revisited* (Grand Rapids, MI: Eerdmans, 2008).

[83] Joseph J. Kotva Jr., "Christian Virtue Ethics and the 'Sectarian Temptation,'" *Heythrop Journal* 35 (1994): 45.

[84] Carson, 224.

[85] H. Richard Niebuhr, *Christ and Culture* (New York: Harper & Brothers, 1951), 11–39. Religious determinations would seem to fit within

the definition of what Niebuhr calls "culture." In fact, Niebuhr's investigation involves the interpretation and application of "Christ" as it engages "culture-without-Christ" or "aspects-of-culture-distinct-from-Christ." That such explorations become complicated should not be surprising.

[86] I owe to David Faber the challenge to consider whether representatives of Christ and Culture categories can be found within the canon itself, as well as some of the possibilities.

[87] See, for example, *Why Christianity Must Change or Die: A Bishop Speaks to Believers in Exile* (San Francisco, CA: HarperCollins, 1998). Cf. Niebuhr, 112–15.

[88] Examples include the similarities of the Pentateuch's legal material with the surrounding culture, as well as the alignment between portions of Proverbs (22:17–23:11) and the Egyptian text, *The Instruction of Amenemope.*

[89] Jim Wallis, *God's Politics* (San Francisco, CA: HarperSanFrancisco, 2005), ch. 3.

[90] In Niebuhr's final chapter, however, he notes that "the types are by no means wholly exclusive of each other, and that there are possibilities of reconciliation at many points among the various positions" (231). Further, he insists that it is not possible to give "*the* Christian answer" to the issue at hand (232).

[91] Niebuhr, 45.

[92] Niebuhr, 67.

[93] Essenes are not mentioned by name in the Bible, though some scholars believe John the Baptist spent time with this group (cf. Matt. 3:1-6; Mark 1:1-6).

[94] For an overview of Western cultural history on this issue, see Lee Hardy, *The Fabric of This World* (Grand Rapids, MI: Eerdmans, 1990), 3–43.

[95] Miller, *Ecclesiastes*, 269–70.

[96] We might therefore consider that John the Baptist's challenge to soldiers—to avoid extortion and false accusation—is not an affirmation of that profession if done correctly, but first steps toward leaving it (Luke 3:14).

[97] That is, slavery in Paul's day should not be confused with the racist and abusive institution that it was in the United States during the seventeenth to nineteenth centuries. Rather, though to be avoided if possible, it was closer to job employment in our time.

[98] New Line Cinema, 2002.

[99] "Work," Merriam-Webster's 11th Collegiate Dictionary, definition 1.

[100] Miroslav Volf, *Work in the Spirit: Toward a Theology of Work* (New York: Oxford University Press, 1991), 10–11.

[101] Disability is a complex issue not discussed here. Many so-called disabled persons have been able to find avenues for their significant gifts and abilities.

[102] Of course, some have the vocation of parenthood in addition to another vocation, suggesting the possibility of duplex (or more) vocations.

[103] Adapted from Smith, *Courage and Calling*, 2nd ed., 49–51.

[104] Keith Graber Miller, *Living Faith: Embracing God's Callings* (Telford, PA: Cascadia, 2012). Also note the sources cited there.

[105] Graber Miller, see esp. ch. 3.

[106] Graber Miller, see esp. ch. 4.

[107] Graber Miller, 50, from C. Arnold Snyder, *Anabaptist History and Theology: An Introduction* (Kitchener, ON: Pandora, 1995), 248.

[108] Adapted from N. T. Wright, "How Can the Bible Be Authoritative?" *Vox Evangelica*, no. 21 (1991): 7–32.

[109] Smith, ch. 5 in *Courage and Calling*, 2nd ed.

[110] Martin Luther King Jr., "The Three Dimensions of a Complete Life," in *A Knock at Midnight: Inspiration from the Great Sermons of Reverend Martin Luther King, Jr.* Ed. by Clayborne Carson and Peter Holloran (New York: Warner, 1998).

[111] Christine and Tom Sine, *Living on Purpose*, 77–89.

[112] Palmer, *Let Your Life Speak*, 6.

[113] Frederick Buechner, *Wishful Thinking: A Seeker's ABC*, rev. and expanded ed. (San Francisco, CA: HarperOne, 1993), 118–19.

[114] The latter is explained by Gordon Lawrence in *People Types and Tiger Stripes*, 3rd ed. (Gainesville, FL: CAPT, 1993).

[115] C. S. Lewis, "Learning in War Time," in *The Weight of Glory and Other Addresses* (New York: Macmillan, 1980), 25.

[116] Richard Foster, *Celebration of Discipline* (San Francisco, CA: Harper and Row, 1978), 96.

Bibliography

Adams, Richard. *Watership Down*. London: Rex Collings, 1972.

Banks, Robert. *Paul's Idea of Community*. 2nd ed. Peabody, MA: Hendrickson, 1994.

Barber, Benjamin R. *Jihad vs. McWorld*, with 2001 Introduction. New York: Ballantine, 1995.

Bates, Matthew W. *Salvation by Allegiance Alone: Rethinking Faith, Works, and the Gospel of Jesus the King*. Grand Rapids, MI: Baker Academic, 2017.

Blackaby, Henry T., and Claude V. King. *Experiencing God*. Nashville, TN: Broadman and Holman, 1994.

Bonhoeffer, Dietrich, *The Cost of Discipleship*. 2d ed. New York: Macmillan, 1959.

Buechner, Frederick. *Wishful Thinking: A Seeker's ABC*. Rev. and expanded ed. San Francisco, CA: HarperOne, 1993.

Carson, D. A. *Christ and Culture Revisited*. Grand Rapids, MI: Eerdmans, 2008.

Carter, Craig A. *Rethinking* Christ and Culture*: A Post-Christendom Perspective*. Grand Rapids, MI: Brazos, 2006.

Chesterton, G. K. *What's Wrong with the World*. London: Cassell, 1910.

Confession of Faith: Commentary and Pastoral Application (Mennonite Brethren). Winnipeg, MB: Kindred, 2000.

Copenhaver, Martin B. *Jesus Is the Question*. Nashville, TN: Abingdon, 2014.

Davidson, Robert. *The Courage to Doubt: Exploring an Old Testament Theme*. London: SCM, 1983

_____. *Wisdom and Worship*. London: SCM, 1990.

Dewey, John. *Reconstruction in Philosophy*. New York: Henry Holt, 1920.

Dulles, Avery. "The Meaning of Faith Considered in Relationship to Justice." In *The Faith That Does Justice: Examining the Christian Sources for Social Change*, edited by John C. Haughey, 10–46. New York: Paulist, 1977.

Flew, Antony. *There Is a God: How the World's Most Notorious Atheist Changed His Mind*. New York: HarperOne, 2007.

Foster, Richard. *Celebration of Discipline*. San Francisco, CA: Harper and Row, 1978.

Friesen, Duane K. *Artists, Citizens, Philosophers: Seeking the Peace of the City*. Scottdale, PA: Herald, 2000.

Graber Miller, Keith. *Living Faith: Embracing God's Callings*. Telford, PA: Cascadia, 2012.

Grimsrud, Ted. *God's Healing Strategy: An Introduction to the Bible's Main Themes*. Rev. ed. Telford, PA: Cascadia, 2011.

Groome, Thomas H. *Christian Religious Education: Sharing Our Story and Vision*. San Francisco, CA: Harper & Row, 1980.

Guinness, Os. *The Call: Finding and Fulfilling the Central Purpose of Your Life*. Nashville, TN: Word, 1998.

Hallie, Philip P. *Lest Innocent Blood Be Shed*. New York: Harper & Row, 1979.

Hardy, Lee. *The Fabric of This World*. Grand Rapids, MI: Eerdmans, 1990.

Hauerwas, Stanley. "A Story-Formed Community: Reflections on *Watership Down*." In *A Community of Character*, 9–35. Notre Dame: University of Notre Dame Press, 1981.

Hays, Richard B. *The Moral Vision of the New Testament: Community, Cross, New Creation: A Contemporary Introduction to New Testament Ethics*. San Francisco, CA: HarperSanFrancisco, 1996.

Hughs, Richard T. *Myths America Lives By*. Urbana and Chicago: University of Illinois Press, 2004.

James, William. *The Will to Believe and Other Essays in Popular Philosophy*. New York: Dover Publications, 1956.

Jenson, Robert W. "How the World Lost Its Story." *First Things* 36 (October 1993): 19–24.

Jones, Howard. *Mutiny on the* Amistad: *The Saga of a Slave Revolt and its Impact on American Abolition, Law, and Diplomacy*. New York: Oxford University Press, 1987.

Keller, Timothy, and Katherine Leary Alsdorf. *Every Good Endeavor: Connecting Your Work to God's Work*. New York: Riverhead, 2012.

Kern, Kathleen. *In Harm's Way: A History of Christian Peacemaker Teams*. Eugene, OR: Cascade, 2009.

King, Martin Luther, Jr. "The Three Dimensions of a Complete Life." In Clayborne Carson and Peter Holloran, eds., *A Knock at Midnight: Inspiration from the Great Sermons of Reverend Martin Luther King, Jr.* New York: Warner, 1998.

Kotva, Joseph J., Jr. *The Christian Case for Virtue Ethics.* Washington, DC: Georgetown University Press, 1997.

_____. "Christian Virtue Ethics and the 'Sectarian Temptation,'" *Heythrop Journal* 35 (1994): 35–42.

Kreeft, Peter. *The Journey: A Spiritual Roadmap for Modern Pilgrims.* Downers Grove, IL: InterVarsity, 1996.

_____. *A Refutation of Moral Relativism: Interviews with an Absolutist.* San Francisco, CA: Ignatius, 1999.

Kreider, Alan. *The Patient Ferment of the Early Church: The Improbable Rise of Christianity in the Roman Empire.* Grand Rapids, MI: Baker Academic, 2016.

Lakoff, George, and Mark Johnson. *Metaphors We Live By.* 2nd ed. Chicago: University of Chicago Press, 2003.

Lawrence, Gordon. *People Types and Tiger Stripes.* 3rd ed. Gainesville, FL: CAPT, 1993.

Leininger, Thomas B. "Scripture & Ethics," lecture notes. Regis University, Denver, Colorado.

Levine, Amy-Jill. *The Misunderstood Jew: The Church and the Scandal of the Jewish Jesus.* San Francisco, CA: HarperSanFrancisco, 2006.

Lewis, C. S. "Learning in War Time." In *The Weight of Glory and Other Addresses.* New York: Macmillan, 1980.

_____. *Mere Christianity.* New York: Macmillan, 1952.

_____. *The Pilgrim's Regress.* 3rd ed. Grand Rapids, MI: Eerdmans, 1943.

_____. *Surprised by Joy.* New York: Harcourt, Brace, and World, 1955.

MacDonald, Gordon. *Ordering Your Private World.* Rev. ed. Nashville, TN: Thomas Nelson, 2003.

MacIntyre, Alasdair. *After Virtue: A Study in Moral Theory.* 3rd ed. Notre Dame, IN: University of Notre Dame Press, 2007.

Martens, Elmer A. *God's Design: A Focus on Old Testament Theology.* 4th ed. Eugene, OR: Wipf & Stock, 2015.

McKnight, Scot. *One.Life: Jesus Calls, We Follow.* Grand Rapids, MI: Zondervan, 2010.

Migliore, Daniel L. *Faith Seeking Understanding: An Introduction to Christian Theology.* 3rd ed. Grand Rapids, MI: Eerdmans, 2014.

Miller, Douglas B. *Ecclesiastes*. Believers Church Bible Commentary. Scottdale, PA: Herald, 2010.
_____. "Will Jonah Be Saved?" in *Beautiful upon the Mountains: Biblical Essays on Mission, Peace, and the Reign of God*, 77-98. Elkhart, IN: Institute of Mennonite Studies, 2003.
Minear, Paul S. *Images of the Church in the New Testament*. Philadelphia, PA: Westminster, 1960.
Mowat, Farley. *Never Cry Wolf*. Atlantic–Little, Brown, 1963.
Newbigin, Leslie. *The Gospel in a Pluralist Society*. Grand Rapids, MI: Eerdmans, 1989.
Niebuhr, H. Richard. *Christ and Culture*. New York: Harper & Brothers, 1951.
Nouwen, Henri J. M. *The Wounded Healer*. New York: Image, 1979.
Palmer, Parker J. *Let Your Life Speak*. San Francisco, CA: Jossey-Bass, 2000.
_____. *To Know as We Are Known*. San Francisco, CA: Harper & Row, 1983.
Peterson, Eugene H. *Working the Angles: The Shape of Pastoral Ministry*. Grand Rapids, MI: Eerdmans, 1987.
Rau, Gerald. *Mapping the Origins Debate*. Downers Grove, IL: InterVarsity, 2012.
Schuurman, Douglas J. *Vocation: Discerning Our Callings in Life*. Grand Rapids, MI: Eerdmans, 2004.
Sine, Christine and Tom. *Living on Purpose: Finding God's Best for Your Life*. Grand Rapids, MI: Baker, 2002.
Sine, Tom. *The Mustard Seed Conspiracy*. Waco, TX: Word, 1981.
_____. *Mustard Seed versus McWorld: Reinventing Life and Faith for the Future*. Grand Rapids, MI: Baker, 1999.
Sire, James W. *Naming the Elephant: Worldview as a Concept*. 2d ed. Downers Grove, IL: InterVarsity, 2015.
_____. *The Universe Next Door: A Basic Worldview Catalog*. 5th ed. Downers Grove, IL: InterVarsity, 2009.
Smith, Christian, et al. *Lost in Transition: The Dark Side of Emerging Adulthood*. New York: Oxford University Press, 2011.
Smith, Gordon T. *Courage and Calling*. 2nd ed. Downers Grove, IL: InterVarsity, 2011.
Snyder, C. Arnold. *Anabaptist History and Theology: An Introduction*. Kitchener, ON: Pandora, 1995.
Spong, John Shelby. *Why Christianity Must Change or Die: A Bishop Speaks to Believers in Exile*. San Francisco, CA: HarperCollins, 1998.

Stassen, Glen H., D. M. Yeager, and John Howard Yoder. *Authentic Transformation: A New Vision of Christ and Culture*. Nashville, TN: Abingdon, 1996.

Stassen, Glen H., and David P. Gushee. *Kingdom Ethics: Following Jesus in Contemporary Context*. 2nd ed. Grand Rapids, MI: Eerdmans, 2016.

Taylor, Daniel. *Tell Me a Story: The Life-Shaping Power of Our Stories*. St. Paul, MN: Bog Walk, 2001.

Tokes, Laszlo, and David Porter. *The Fall of Tyrants*. Wheaton, IL: Crossway, 1990.

Volf, Miroslav. *Work in the Spirit: Toward a Theology of Work*. New York: Oxford University Press, 1991.

Wallis, Jim. *God's Politics*. San Francisco, CA: HarperSanFrancisco, 2005.

Walsh, Brian J., and J. Richard Middleton. *The Transforming Vision: Shaping a Christian Worldview*. Downers Grove, IL: Inter-Varsity, 1984.

Whitney, Donald S. *Spiritual Disciplines for the Christian Life*. Colorado Springs, CO: NavPress, 1991.

Wilkens, Steve, and Mark L. Sanford. *Hidden Worldviews: Eight Cultural Stories that Shape Our Lives*. Downers Grove, IL: Inter-Varsity, 2009.

Willard, Dallas. *The Spirit of the Disciplines*. San Francisco, CA: Harper and Row, 1989.

Wisdom, John. "Gods." In John Hick, ed., *Classical and Contemporary Readings in the Philosophy of Religion*. Engelwood Cliffs, NJ: Prentice-Hall, 1964.

Wolterstorff, Nicholas. *Until Justice and Peace Embrace*. Grand Rapids, MI: Eerdmans, 1983.

Wright, N. T. "How Can the Bible Be Authoritative?" *Vox Evangelica*, no. 21 (1991): 7–32.

_____. *Jesus and the Victory of God*. London: SPCK, 1996.

_____. *Simply Christian: Why Christianity Makes Sense*. San Francisco, CA: HarperCollins, 2006.

Yoder, Bob. *Helping Youth Grieve: The Good News of Biblical Lament*. Eugene, OR: Wipf & Stock, 2015.

Yoder, Perry B. *Shalom: The Bible's Word for Salvation, Justice, and Peace*. Newton, KS: Faith and Life, 1987.

Index

The Author

Douglas Miller serves as professor of biblical and religious studies at Tabor College, Hillsboro, Kansas, where he teaches courses in biblical studies and faith in contemporary culture. He is a graduate of Oral Roberts University, Anabaptist Mennonite Biblical Seminary, and Princeton Theological Seminary, where he earned a Ph.D. in Old Testament.

Miller has published articles in church and scholarly periodicals and contributed essays to published collections. He served as general editor of *Direction* journal for ten years, as editor of *Tabor College: A Century of Transformation* (centennial history book), and is currently Old Testament editor of the Believers Church Bible Commentary series and the online *Anabaptist Dictionary of the Bible* project. His published books include *Symbol and Rhetoric in Ecclesiastes* (Society of Biblical Literature/E. J. Brill), *Ecclesiastes* (BCBC, Herald Press), and *An Akkadian Handbook* (with R. Mark Shipp, Eisenbrauns).

Miller lives in Hillsboro, Kansas. He is married to Holly Swartzendruber, is the father of three adult married sons, and has several grandchildren.